ADVANCED PRAISE FOR AMERICAN BADASS

"It was George Orwell who stated, "People sleep peacefully at night because rough men stand ready to do violence on her behalf." That quote from Orwell adequately describes a true American warrior, Dale Comstock. Dale's book *American Badass* chronicles the story of a man who has dedicated his entire life to the defense of our freedoms, liberty, and way of life. Dale is truly an exceptional soldier. He is possibly the youngest ever to qualify for the Special Forces Operations Detachment Delta, the premier US counter-terrorism unit. However, it is not just his military accomplishments, but his drive for excellence in every aspect of his life, that put him a cut above the rest. Dale Comstock represents the legacy and lineage of service to America, from his dad who served in Vietnam to his son who now serves. *American Badass* is the story of something rare—a modern day Spartan."

—Allen B. West, former US representative,
Lieutenant Colonel (US Army, retired)

"The first time I ever met Dale Comstock, I had to fight him. Fortunately, it was for a film sequence, but it was obvious that I was trading blows with the real deal, an authentic warrior, a true badass. I've fought a ton of guys onscreen... stunt guys... ex-military... MMA fighters... but my fight with Dale was by far the most nervous I've ever been. It was like fighting a tree... a scary, killer oak. Even then, it wasn't until I read this book that I came to understand what a genuine AMERICAN BADASS Dale really is. From his patriotic service as Delta Force operator to his commitment as a husband and father, Dale's incredible story represents the very best of what it means to be an American... and a man."

– Christian Kane, actor, singer/songwriter

"Unlike many books written today by government operators, Comstock's book isn't a guns-a- blazing, kill-everything-in-sight, romanticized-war book. It is a book about character, patriotism, humility, love, and a calling.

"Comstock does an exceptional job revealing the true person he is—cocky, arrogant, fearless, yet caring, humble, loyal, and, most of all, loving. He demonstrates through his writing that he truly is America's warrior—well rounded, tough, and committed to seeing the mission completed, whether it be in combat or on a Hollywood set. In his book Dale makes himself out to be an *American Badass*, but with good reason—he is one.

"Dale is a highly trained government operator who served in Panama, Iraq, and Afghanistan, along with other unique hot-spots around the globe. Throughout Dale's book, he does something very few have ever done. Sure, he explains what life was like growing up, what life was like making it through the Delta and Special Forces selections, but none of that is what makes Dale's book so brilliant—through his book, Dale made me want to get back into the fight and strive to be a better husband, writer, daddy, and person.

"If I had all the money in the world, I would give a copy of *American Badass* to every expecting father, every gangbanger, and surely every soldier, sailor, airman, and Marine. *American Badass* is a must read!"

> – Kerry Patton, a combat-disabled veteran, is author of
> Contracted: America's Secret Warriors

"When Dale Comstock entered the ranks of Delta Force he was told, "Run the situation, don't let the situation run you." In *American Badass*, odds-beater Comstock always runs the edges—hair-on-fire and full-throttle—into some of the most unforgiving and jacked-up places in the world. If the US Constitution had a 28th Amendment it would read: If diplomacy fails and war is inevitable, declare it quick, and send Comstock!"

> – Dalton Fury, former Delta Force operator and two-time
> New York Times bestselling author

This book was made possible by the tremendous support of:

Chris Wilson
Mark Viracola
Stephan Shelanski

Thank you.

AMERICAN BADASS

The true story of a modern day Spartan

Dale Comstock

Zulu 7

AMERICAN BADASS
THE TRUE STORY OF A MODERN DAY SPARTAN

American Badass © 2013 Zulu 7 Productions, LLC, Zulu 7 Media LLC, and Dale Comstock.

ISBN-10: 0989483509
ISBN-13: 978-0-9894835-0-6

To request a review copy for an article or to interview the author, please visit www.DaleComstock.com
and www.Zulu7Publishing.com.

Cover Design by Jennifer Welker

Published by Zulu 7 Media in association with Quiet Owl Books.

American Badass is available for bulk purchases at special discounts for schools, organizations, and special events. For more information please contact books@zulu7publishing.com

Dedicated to:

MSG (R) Michael W. Donatelli
1967−2013
Ranger, Green Beret, Delta Force

Contents

FOREWORD

I wrote this book on the urging of many friends and associates. In fact, I made my decision to write the book in September 2012 while I was on the set of *Stars Earns Stripes*, speaking with Chris Kyle, the author of *American Sniper*. As we discussed his book, he looked at me and said to everyone nearby—"I am waiting to read your book, Dale." It was at that point I decided it was time to write.

I didn't want the book to just be about me and my combat experiences. I wanted to reach out to our young men, young women, fathers, and mothers and tell them a story about successful parenting and what I think it means to succeed on personal merit, hard work, and sacrifice. I decided to use my life experiences as the medium to mentor. I find myself in a country where traditional values are being replaced by a prevailing and metastasizing sense of entitlement, where hard work and personal excellence are no longer the cornerstones for success, where young men and boys have become apathetic and their heroes are virtual characters in video games, where street football is played out on a couch in front of a wide screen TV whilst many look to their left and right and see their fathers, who should be their mentors, life coaches, and leaders, lying on the couch, overweight, or feet propped up in a recliner, beckoning the wife to fetch another beer and bag of chips!

My competitors from the NBC show *Stars Earn Stripes* bestowed the moniker American Badass upon me. An American Badass can be a man or woman. One only needs to be a role model and lead by positive example. An American Badass doesn't start fights, but knows if he must fight, he can with courage and conviction. An American Badass doesn't steal, lie, or subvert the society that he lives in. He lives by a code of unwavering morality, and ethics that are tempered with honor, honesty, integrity, leadership, and loyalty to family, friends, and America.

We have become a society so bent on finding Utopia that we are ignoring the realities of the world. There is no Utopia. We live in a world that will never be at peace. The fact that mankind has fought over 12,000 wars since the beginning of our existence is a good indicator that we will never realize total peace. Segments of our society have been working fervently over the last two decades in the name of political correctness to neuter our young men. Boys are discouraged from fighting in self-defense, from making verbal advances toward girls, from playing with toy guns. Instead, they're encouraged to play with dolls to evoke their sensitive sides. We have become a nation that expects our teachers to raise our children, and the government to take care of our basic needs; a culture that reveres athletes and the winners of *American Idol* and all but ignores the sacrifices police, first-responders, and military members make.

I earned a doctorate degree in alternative medicine and a master's in business and security management while I boxed professionally, concurrently serving in the Army and married, with three children. I have been in every ground combat operation from Grenada to Afghanistan and Iraq as an infantryman, Special Operations soldier, and paramilitary contractor for the government. I have participated in hundreds of combat operations, including the famed raid on Modelo Prison, and was twice decorated for valor.

American Badass is a story inspired by my journey from boyhood to manhood, from innocence to a world of extreme violence, from a paltry and humble existence to a life enriched through determination, hard work, sacrifice, and the love of family. It is the story of the road less traveled—of failure and success by a Delta Force operator, a Green Beret, a husband, a father, and...an American.

DISCLAIMER

When I wrote this book I wanted to ensure that in no way would I compromise operational security. Because I have a legal and moral obligation to guard sensitive information, not including declassified or open source information, I have opted not to use true names of persons and operations, exact times and locations, and I have used alternate names for organizations that I have worked for as a paramilitary contractor after my military service. This book is based on true events.

SPECIAL THANKS

I would like to thank the people in my life who have shaped, guided, mentored, and loved me. A special thanks to my wife, Miroslava, who is the pillar that I lean on; to my children, who have inspired me to be the best example of a father that I can be; to my mother and father, who raised me, taught me, and motivated me to be the best me; to all of my friends, who stood by me and believed in me; to all of my enemies, who galvanized my will to succeed, and to the US Army, who trained me and taught me how to be a good citizen—I say, with all of my heart, thank you.

Of Lions and Lambs

Afghanistan 2003

"You shall not be afraid by the terror of night,
nor of the arrow that flies by day"
—Psalm 91.53

1

The radio crackled and popped before the voice became clear.
"Dale, this is Travis…" the man said.

"Travis, this is Dale. Go!" I responded.

A pause, then, "Roger. My vehicle is INOP. I'm at grid coordinate 234897. How copy?"

"Good copy, Travis," I replied. "I'll pass your grid to the EXFIL bird and call for immediate extraction. Stand by…"

"Roger."

"Dale, this is Joe," another voice chimed on the radio. "I'm 1500 meters west of your position and standing by to assist."

"Joe, Dale—Roger! Mike, this is Dale—SITREP?"

"Dale, DE Mike bird is short-final. I have visual and ready to execute!"

A few moments later and I added, "Travis, I have eyes on your bird. He's inbound—north-south heading, two miles out. Two hundred feet at eighty knots. Stand by for hot EXFIL."

Frost edged the windshield of my vehicle. The desert sky was without clouds or illumination from the moon. Pitch black. Two floodlights were positioned toward the stalled vehicle stopped on the desert road, casting eerie shadows over the sagebrush. It all seemed so surreal.

My mind nearly envisioned Taliban behind every bush, crouching ever closer to finish us off. I was getting tired and I knew Travis was ready to be recovered and get the hell out of this area of operations too.

The sound of crunching metal filled the night air. My voice wavered, but my training took over, and I spoke clearly. "All stations, this is Dale. EXFIL bird has just gone down. Went down hard into the n-s chasm, 300 meters west of Travis's location. Call for emergency dust-off, rescue, and all available hands to assist!" My tone remained steady, not betraying my emotions.

It took a few moments before I received a response. The impossible had happened, and everyone was in shock. Finally, Travis replied, asking, "Dale, did the helicopter just crash?"

"Affirmative," I replied, stoically.

"Tell us what to do," voices in the night begged, panicked voices. "My God, this can't be happening!"

I ran into the mouth of madness, into the darkness of the deadly night. I tore off into the unknown, clearing the crest and descending into the dark chasm. I didn't know what lay ahead, but I bore headfirst. If there was any chance of survival, I'd be there to help them.

I ran down 150 feet. I was alone; one man in the pitch-black night, running toward danger.

The others didn't move. They were frozen in disbelief. They didn't know what to do, their minds, their souls were numb. Some later recalled that the pilot's words repeated in their minds as the helicopter went down. During an earlier safety briefing, he had dissuaded anyone from ever approaching the crash site if the helicopter went down. It was for their protection, of course. The pilot had warned of possible fire hazards, as fuel would no doubt douse the area. There was also the potential deadliness of the spinning rotor blades.

"Do not approach," he had cautioned.

It was not an option.

People could be alive, men who could be saved. And the fear of personal injury didn't factor into my decision as I rushed into the chaos.

2

Being a warrior, one expects death. It comes with the territory. We choose this, though we never wish it.

A soldier must learn to accept death: the loss of a brother-in-arms, the loss of a friend. Over my long career, I've expected tragedy, and I've experienced much of it. But soldiers are trained for this. Our training teaches us to deal with it, to accept it, even if it haunts us forever.

And believe me, it does.

One of the most traumatizing events I have ever experienced was not while in service to this great country, but after I had retired. It was February 2013, and I was working on my next stage in life. My Hollywood career was going well, and I was selected to be on a reality TV show being filmed in northern Los Angeles. The show was intended to honor Special Operations (SPECOPs) soldiers.

It promised to be a good one.

The cast included me and four other stellar American soldiers. These men were the best of the best—two Green Berets, a Delta Force soldier, and a Navy SEAL. There were also approximately forty production crewmembers, and the guys and I did not know what to expect. I was new to this whole Hollywood thing, but the people I was working with were beyond professional, and I felt the show would be a hit.

We had been filming for a few weeks. All was going well, and I was enjoying the process. We filmed long hours, and were working on the final scene. This was the first episode, the pilot, and we wanted it to be great.

It was a Sunday morning, 0333 hours, and cold, only twenty-eight degrees. I cannot express how brutally cold it was. Bone chilling. It was dark out, no moon in the sky, very few lights on the set.

This scene involved off-road driving in the desert. The driver of the car was a Navy SEAL. He was supposed to execute high-speed maneuvers for the scene. During one of the maneuvers, he would abruptly stop. At that time, he would pass grid coordinates to me, and my job was to vector in a helicopter that would hover above the car. The helicopter would then dump a rucksack with special instructions, and we would go on to our next "mission."

Nothing complicated for guys like us, but dangerous nonetheless. Anytime you are attempting to simulate a combat scenario, odds are things will go wrong. Safety is key, and we had some experts around for any contingencies.

I remember the helicopter's pilot saying to us, "If things go wrong, if the bird goes down, stay away."

His point was that it was dangerous. Jet fuel could explode; pieces of metal could go flying. But we expected nothing of the sort. This was just another walk in the park for guys like us.

Originally, I was supposed to fly in the helicopter. My job would be to dump the rucksack to the waiting car below. However, after some discussion with the cast and crew, it was decided I should remain on deck. This suggestion was made by the Delta soldier, Mike Donatelli. The reason was my extensive knowledge of off-road driving, vehicle dynamics, and other technicalities of insane driving. It sounded like a good plan.

The reality of movie-making is this: sometimes the script changes. Sometimes you must improvise, change things to add value to production, to make a scene better.

Whatever the scene called for, we would accomplish the mission. We all wanted this first part to be great. And Mike decided he should be in the air.

This is a choice I will never forget. One that will cause my heart to ache until the day I die.

3

The scene begins.

The SEAL at the wheel drives the car as if he's just stolen it. I'm expecting nothing less. He rips around corners, mashing the gas, pushing the car to its max.

SEALs—gotta love 'em!

While he was doing this, I was supplying the commentary. I was about two hundred meters away, standing in the California desert, in the darkness, in the cold, talking into a microphone. I spoke of the follies of driving such a small car in such a way. I talked of the dangers of such high speeds, especially at night on a dirt desert road.

Though the scene appeared complex, and though the car and helicopter maneuvers seemed complicated, it was all routine. We were all experienced, the pilot being one of the best.

The helicopter began circling, and circling fast. It was flying flat, two hundred feet above the ground, screaming by as it swooped past, doing eighty knots. Again and again it made passes. During this time, I was saying whatever came to mind. Explaining the technique, relaying the mission orders, describing whatever I could think of.

Mostly, I was anxious to get out of the cold.

The scene continued. Once I completed my commentary, and the vehicle stopped, I got inside my SUV so I could warm up. One of the assistant producers hopped in beside me, and we took one last look up at the helicopter as it completed its orbit, flying right before us.

Then, something changed.

The helicopter's nose slanted downward. It tucked below a ridge, heading toward a dry riverbed. I remember mumbling, "That's one crazy dive! That pilot has guts."

Then, I began counting. "…One, two, three…"

I waited for him to pull up. But I knew. I knew there was a problem.

Then I heard it. A deafening noise.

One of the producers looked my way, his face pale in my headlamp, his mouth wide.

"Did it just crash?" he asked.

"Yeah," I replied, my voice grim.

I took off, running as fast as I could.

Headed into the darkness, into chaos.

Headed into the mouth of madness as I'd done so many times before.

4

I sprang from the SUV with the assistant producer on my heels. I remember clearing the crest of the waddy and starting my 150-foot descent in total darkness. Fortunately, I was wearing a coal miner's headlamp to give me some light. Behind me, voices cried out, asking me what they should do.

They had never experienced anything like this before they exclaimed.

I yelled to them to call for the medic, an air Medevac, and the fire department, and to bring fire extinguishers and blankets.

I never slowed down, as all I could think was, "What if there are survivors?"

As I reached the point of impact and saw the wreckage, I had a horrible feeling that no one survived. The crash site was littered with pieces no bigger than shoeboxes. The biggest pieces of wreckage I came across were about two feet of tail boom and a partial shell of the transmission housing.

As I stood there, alone, I pondered where to start my search. The wreckage was strewn about for 300 feet in a cone-shaped configuration in the direction of flight. The fuel tank had erupted and everything was doused in JP-4 jet fuel. My pants and boots were soaked from running through the sagebrush.

I began to scan clockwise when I saw the first casualty at my two o'clock about fifteen feet away.

I ran to him and quickly assessed his condition. Without a doubt, he was beyond saving. His body's state snatched my breath away and made me stand upright to take a deep breath. I will never forget the sight of brain matter on my gloves.

I scanned to my right and spotted the second casualty at my four o'clock about ten feet away, lying between two bushes.

I sprinted to him and, to my shock and horror, he was mortally injured but still breathing. He had suffered, among other things, a traumatic head injury that had compromised the integrity of his skull. His wounds were extensive and he choked on his blood and teeth. I grabbed him by his torso and gently rolled him to his side to clear his airway.

It was as if I had grabbed a bag of marbles.

It was all I could do to hold it together as I yelled for the medic and anyone in earshot to help me.

I called out, "I got two and missing one. Get me a medic. Get me a medic now!"

I didn't want to leave the man I was with because he needed my help to remain breathing.

Suddenly, I heard a woman's voice about fifteen feet behind me. It was a beautiful lady from the production crew, who had shown exceptional fortitude and run out to the crash site to help. She cried out an inaudible sound and hurried away.

At that point, I knew she had found the third casualty. I carefully balanced the second casualty on his side and promised him that I would return quickly. I ran to the third and conducted an initial survey, looking for life. It didn't take long for me to realize he had expired.

When I returned to him, the second casualty was still breathing, but barely.

I cried out with frustration for the medic again. At this point, time slowed down and my head filled with thoughts about this man, his family, and what I could do to save him.

I felt so helpless. The damage was so extensive, I didn't think a team of surgeons operating in optimal conditions could save him. All I could do was plead to him to stay with me. I begged him, "Hang in there, brother! You're going to be okay!"

I knew in my heart that was a lie, but I had to say and do anything that might keep his candle burning.

As I held his body soaked in jet fuel, I watched helplessly as his breaths slowed and then faded to nothing.

He was gone.

Thirty seconds later the medic came running in and quickly went to work. I stood up, surrounded by three bodies, wondering whether this was a dream. I turned and looked at Mike's body as he lay peacefully, and a chill came over me as I realized that it should have been me. I cheated death, again, and Mike was cheated out of life…

Within minutes, my counterpart, Joe, arrived and called out my name, frantically. "Dale, SITREP?"

"They're all gone, Joe. I'm sorry."

Joe and Mike had been best friends for over twenty years.

Though I had been surrounded by over forty-five people that night, most were paralyzed and too in shock to help, but my training, my past experiences, and my love for my fellow man overshadowed any fear one would have over running into a dangerous situation with total abandon. It didn't matter, and I didn't think about it.

I know that the others were not cowards; they were professionals and did all they could do within their experience. I feel sorry for them and the hurt and sorrow they endured. I wish they never had to experience that, and my heart goes out to them, each and every one of them.

I walked away from this experience realizing that all of these years this is what it was all about.

It wasn't about killing the enemy. It was about protecting Americans from the wolf at the door, doing the heavy lifting, cleaning up the mess that for most was too hard to stomach, and it was a privilege to stand between them and death.

Babies and Bullies

My sister and me, 1966

5

I was born in 1963 in Fort Lewis, Washington, to James and Lydia Comstock. My father, who was English and Cherokee Indian, served in Vietnam and was a twenty-year veteran. I was born into military life. My entire childhood was experienced in military society. My mother was of German descent, and she and my father were married for fifty-one years—until my father died in 2012. He suffered a myriad of afflictions, including diseases related to Agent Orange and other chemicals used as defoliants in Vietnam.

Most of my childhood and teenage years were spent in Germany where my father was stationed. I bonded with many other dependent kids and families, and together, we were like an island of Americans in a foreign land. I enjoyed the best of both worlds, given that half of my family was German. However, though I am half-German and fluent in the language, I always considered myself an American.

I had wonderful experiences growing up in military surroundings. My father and my friends' fathers were issued TA-50 gear (tactical military gear), and we would wear their equipment and play army. We would build rubber-band guns and at times shoot each other with BB guns—it was all-out war. Often our sisters and girlfriends joined us. We formed little armies and would play-fight throughout the military housing area for hours.

One time, we built mortars out of old steel soda pop cans—before aluminum became the container of choice. We taped the open ends of the cans together to form a cylinder about three to four feet long. The last can on one end remained sealed with a small slit about one inch from the bottom where we poured rubbing alcohol. A tennis ball, which fit perfectly into the muzzle at the other end, was inserted and rammed two-thirds of the way down the pipe. Once we acquired a target, a lighter would fire up the alcohol at the ignition port. Once fired, making an impressive sound and flash, the mortar would launch the tennis ball at least 300 yards at an incredible rate. The longer the tube and the more alcohol used, the greater the range and velocity.

As cool as it was to launch mortars at each other, the thrill soon waned as we found ourselves on an Easter egg hunt, looking for our limited supply of tennis balls each time. The lesson learned? Use a direct-fire weapon sparingly (for psychological effect mainly), and ensure you have some kind of backstop so the ball doesn't travel too far if you miss. No surprise, I grew up to become a light-and-heavy weapons expert in Special Forces (SF).

Football, street or tackle, without pads was another perennial favorite. I remember playing for hours in the mud, fog, and winter slush every day after school. We played until the sun went down and our mothers hollered out of apartment windows for us to come home, eat dinner, and get ready for bed. All of the neighborhood kids would play, including the girls. This was no tag football—it was all-out tackle, the mission to plow down the guy or gal with the ball. If a player got up moaning and crying, there was a good chance he would end up with the ball again.

We would run him down like a pack of hyenas until he toughened up or went home to Mommy. No anti-bullying law was going to save his ass from the wrath of his peers if he didn't grab his ball sack (or put down his purse) and stand his ground. If a player didn't like a call or had a problem, it was resolved on the field—sometimes with a fistfight. When it was over, everyone went back to playing football and remained friends.

What I loved most was how we would score points against each other and at the end of the day we, as a group, accepted our losses and winnings, and came back the next day to play just as hard. We learned to pick teams fairly, play fairly, fight fairly, and win and lose fairly. There was no "sissification" of the game. Unlike in many sports today, there were winners and losers. If you lost, it was because you were not the best, and you sure as hell didn't deserve a trophy for that. When I was growing up, a person's feelings of inadequacy were not everyone's concern. They were a personal issue to either cope with or grow out of.

It seems to me that in the '70s and early '80s kids were tougher. Opinions on this matter abound, but I think part of the reason is we weren't coddled like many of today's kids. Today's kids are overwhelmed with electronics, texting, and the Internet. They are, in some ways, socially inept. If kids today would get off the couch and find their way to the front door (wearing sneakers, not flip-flops), they would enter a world that is as foreign as Mars. I doubt most have ever gotten into street fights, chased girls, or played ball games in vacant lots. Kids who won't walk outside if it's raining because their hair might get wet surround me. It makes me shake my head and think, What in the hell?

The Patriarchs

My father in his dress greens uniform out of basic training

My German uncle and my German grandfather, Opa.

The three most influential men in my life.

6

My father was my hero. He raised me to be a man and to act like a man, and that was expected of me even as a boy. I was a little guy starting out in life. Though, interestingly, my father and mother were both 5'4", I ended up inheriting height from my mother's family and bulk from my father's side, yielding a 5'11" and 210-pound frame—or combat chassis, as I like to say. My dad was a good father who treated my only sister and me fairly. He was kind but firm and always there for us, his reliance a quality that I try very hard to imitate when dealing with my children.

The one thing that I believe most shaped my character and taught me to never quit was my father's winning attitude. As I mentioned, I was a runt growing up, right up to basic training in the Army. When I enlisted, I weighed a total of 143 pounds. Now, I was light, but I was by no means a pushover. Growing up, I was often the target for larger bullies. In fact, I like to think that I was a handsome young man who attracted the attention of many girls, and, consequently, a lot of jealous guys who wanted to punk me out and embarrass me in front of the ladies.

What bullies didn't expect was that my father and mother were tenacious people who didn't tolerate me getting beat up. Their intolerance, however, was not directed at my enemies— rather, it was directed at me.

My parents didn't go out and admonish other kids; they would threaten me with a worse beating if I lost a fight.

Talk about pressure! I have had well over two hundred fights in my life, ranging from a face-off with a pissed-off five-year-old to a war with a gang of five teenagers that wanted to beat me down. No matter how scared I was, or how much I didn't want to fight, if my father was around, he made it very clear that running home or getting beat was not an option for me.

I remember one night me and this other kid were fighting under a street light over a girl—I know it was silly, but it was fun—and my father walked out of the house and saw the battle. I was on top of the guy, raining tiny punches down on his head.

My father walked up to us, and he said to me as he sipped from a can of his favorite beer, "You better kick his ass, son, or don't come home!"

He then walked off and left my opponent and me to continue our engagement. I'm not sure where he went or what he did after, but I got the job done and neither of us got the girl.

The next day, the boy and I were friends, and within a few more days, we had our next battle in the public swimming pool…over another girl.

Whenever I fought, my dad always seemed to show up and sternly remind me that I'm a Comstock and that we don't run and we don't lose. And if we lose, it's not from lack of trying. To be fair, my parents also taught me to not start trouble—they taught me restraint, discretion, and judicial use of force—but when trouble came about, they wanted me to know that I didn't have to be abused or hurt.

I remember when I was ten years old, walking with my German grandfather (my Opa) through the American housing area in Stuttgart, Germany. It was obvious to anyone looking that my Opa was German, and I looked German as well.

Some American boys were playing next to a few cars on the road. Suddenly, and without warning, one of the boys ran out, punched me in the face, and then darted. He struck me because he thought I was German, and he was being hateful. Without hesitation, I ran after the boy and caught him. I threw him against a car and reared my fist back to return the hit.

But before I released my punch, I looked over at my grandfather, a big man with a bald head like mine is now, as he stood in the spot where I was struck, with his hands in his coat pockets. The look in his eyes told me that I had already won and that I had no reason to continue the fight. I released the boy as I stared into my Opa's eyes, and I walked back to him.

We never discussed what happened; we continued our quiet walk, because all of the questions that one would want answered were already answered and the lesson had been learned.

Now what does this all say about me?

What it says is that my parents, especially the patriarchs close to me – my father and Opa, taught me to take care of myself through forceful assertion, strong will, and prudence. They taught me the mental and emotional skills necessary to cope with and vanquish my fears. What they did not do was instill a false sense of security by overprotecting me. They knew they couldn't always be there for me and that, if I was to acclimate to the world, I would need to be prepared for both the good and the bad.

Autogenic Conditioning—
The Mind Game

What the dreams of men can conceive, the will of man can achieve.

7

When I was a kid I accidently learned a lesson that most human beings on earth never have. Coupled with the lessons my parents taught me about protecting myself, it has brought me success and confidence in everything I do.

At fourteen, I played baseball for the Dependent Youth Activity (DYA) in Stuttgart. In my neighborhood, we had two teams: the Pattonville All Stars and the Pattonville Royals. All the "good" players ended up on the All Stars and all of the "not so good" players ended up on the Royals. During that era, the movie *Bad News Bears* had been released, and the Royals were given that moniker.

So, what team was I selected for? You guessed it—the Royals. I gotta admit, I was a terrible baseball player. I usually played left field and sometimes I played "left out" on the bench.

Now, what I could do well was throw that baseball like a bullet—I just couldn't catch it very well. At least in left field, the ball usually rolled to me, so all I had to do was scoop it up. My poor skills were mostly the by-product of my inexperience and, thus, my lack of confidence.

One sunny Saturday, our team played the All Stars and we were beaten badly. Moreover, our only catcher was kicked in the groin. We were scheduled to compete against the All Stars again the following Saturday. On the following Friday, our coach got word that our catcher was permanently out, and he needed to find a replacement.

Now, I have no idea why this happened, but my coach decided that I would be the catcher for the next game against the All Stars. My first thought was that this guy was a prick who was trying to humiliate me to death.

I had less than thirty minutes to practice that afternoon, but being the trooper that I am, I was prepared to face any challenge, regardless of how scared I was. I practiced and listened to all of the advice that a baseball team could give me in half an hour.

After practice, I went home and contemplated the situation. I was nervous as hell and decided I had to do something to better prepare myself for the next morning. But what could I do? It was evening, dark outside; my friends were home and there was no other practical way to prepare…or was there?

That night I learned something that would forever change my life. During that era, it was unheard of. In fact, most people today have never heard of it, and those who have, have a very vague understanding of the concept. Some people call it visualization, but that's too simplistic.

The scientific term is autogenic conditioning. It's the practice of visualizing a task over and over exactly the way it is to be performed until one can execute the task physically as well as it was rehearsed in the mind.

Both the right side of the brain, which controls imagination, and the left side, which controls willpower, are at play here. They oppose each other in that the right side wants to avoid potential pain and the left side wants to seek pleasure. The right side tends to win out, because we are more inclined to avoid pain than to seek pleasure, especially when it comes to something we are not familiar with.

A medical doctor named Emile Coué was more or less the founding father of this theory, which originated in the 1920s. Coué's Law states: "Whenever imagination and willpower are in conflict, imagination will inevitably win."

So, what does all that mean? Your performance is based on your inherent potential and your ability to cope with stress. If you can't cope with stress related to a task, you're not going to be very successful. In any training course that I teach, I explain to my students that stress is an inability to cope.

One can learn to cope experientially, by practicing a task in the same conditions that one would expect to execute it when the time came.

Another way to gain experience, and thus confidence, is to simulate the environment, conditions, and tasks in your mind. This mental rehearsal must resemble the actual experience (consider the sights, sounds, and feelings) as closely as possible in order for you to learn successfully.

That night before the match against the All Stars I went to bed around seven. I put my headphones on and started to listen to my favorite music. I closed my eyes, relaxed, and then imagined myself playing catcher in the game. I visualized everything from catching the ball and feeling its impact in my mitt to swinging the bat across my field of view. I saw myself doing everything from scooping up dirt-balls that skimmed across the plate to doffing my mask and catching pop flies. I imagined making double plays and not letting one ball get behind me at the plate. I sensed the dust, the fans yelling, the breeze, the smells—everything that would interact with the senses on that impending day. Most importantly, I executed every movement perfectly over and over, until I fell asleep about five hours later.

The next morning I was one of the first players to arrive at the baseball field. I donned my equipment, took my post behind home plate, and practiced with the pitcher. I still vividly remember parents arriving and then, to my dismay, questioning me as to why I was playing catcher. The discouragement didn't end there, as these adults went en mass and openly complained to my coach.

It was, to say the least, very humiliating for me. My coach, who was a gangly and gentle man, displayed a pair of balls bigger than an elephant that day: he stood behind me, and his decision, and told the parents to sit in the bleachers and enjoy the sunshine.

Now, if this were a movie, the theme song to *Rocky* or *The Flight of the Valkyries* would have been playing in the background.

That day I didn't allow one pitch to escape me, one ball to drop, not one runner to score. I single-handedly made several double plays by catching pop-ups and throwing out the runner at second and third base.

On that glorious day, I was a one-man baseball team. I walked away with the game ball and the title of most valuable player. In five hours of meditation, I transformed from a caterpillar to a butterfly. I went from being the worst athlete on the team to the best, and I maintained that standing for the rest of the years that I played baseball.

Ranger Up

High School 1981, Basic Training

8

In the beginning of my senior year of high school, I received a phone call from an Army recruiter by the name of Staff Sergeant Dobbins, who invited me to his office to discuss career options in the Army. Now, I have to tell you here that I was a terrible student, and I had just finished summer school after having realized on my own that I didn't have enough credits to graduate high school unless I went to summer school and caught up.

What made my summer worse was that, at the end of my junior year, I had broken my right arm playing basketball. I snapped my arm near the wrist slam-dunking the basketball. Yes, I slam-dunked the ball at 5'11". I was one hell of an athlete and could jump like a kangaroo. I had to complete all of my summer school writing assignments with my left hand although I'm a right-handed writer. I was getting so burned out with school that the prospect of four more years of college didn't appeal to me in the least.

I decided to go to the recruiter's office and hear him out.

SSG Dobbins was a short, redheaded Irishman, with the wit of a comic. As I sat across his desk, I listened and watched as he laid an array of literature about electronics and technical occupations in front of me. He went on to give me his best sales pitch about careers in these areas. I listened until I couldn't take it anymore. I finally said, "Stop, Staff Sergeant Dobbins. Tell me about Airborne Rangers!"

I had recently seen an advertisement in the local *TV Guide* of an Army Ranger coming out of the tree line with camouflage on his face, wearing a patrol cap, a rappel rope slung over his shoulder as he carried a CAR-15. He looked badass! And I knew then that was who I wanted to be.

SSG Dobbins looked up at me with a surprised look on his face, likely because I was a small guy, weighing in at a whopping 143 pounds. I guess I looked more like a nerd than a steely-eyed killer. But that didn't keep him from wiping his desk clean with one brush of his arm and presenting a single pamphlet about the size of a post card. It looked so simple compared to all the technical data that he had laid out that it didn't take any convincing on his part that I should be a Ranger.

My only question was, When can I go and do I pay you for this?

After I enlisted, my two best friends, Joe and Ken, were so excited that they enlisted too. Because we had all signed up at once, we were immediately promoted to Private 2nd Class, and we didn't even own uniforms yet! It made us feel superior until we went into service and realized we were pretty much at the bottom of the military social ladder.

I remember when I announced to my parents what I had done, and the reaction that I didn't get. My mother didn't say much, but my father was disappointed about my choice, especially since I didn't confer with him first.

My father—the twenty-year soldier—knew more than what I thought I knew about what I was getting into.

Moreover, he told me that he really hoped that I would go to college. No one at that time had been to college on either side of my family. My father had an eleventh grade education and my mother had what amounted to a ninth grade education. He wanted me to be the first to break the ceiling and get that coveted college degree.

I heard the pain and anguish in his voice, and I realized that I should have talked to my parents before enlisting. Talking to them would not have changed my mind, but I would have felt better knowing I had given them a chance to express their feelings. The decision was made and the damage done, however. All I could do was try to find a compromise and hope that I would get my father's blessing.

My compromise was the promise that I would not only make him proud of me as a soldier but also earn my college degree.

I didn't let my father down. I respected my parents and all they did for my sister and me, the love they gave us, the upbringing and family life they immersed us in.

While I was in service, I spent most of my career humping a rucksack and kicking in doors. I was a field soldier who didn't enjoy the comforts of an office or some other job that kept me home and out of the field (with the exception of eighteen months where I was assigned as the 3rd Special Forces Group's assistant operations and training NCO).

Eventually, I managed to earn my bachelor's and master's degrees while in service, which was a lesson in not letting anyone tell me that I couldn't do something. I used to listen to soldiers—especially Special Forces soldiers—tell me that, because of the job, they didn't have time to go to college.

No one said that it was going to be easy. In fact, it was hard as hell going to school and constantly being deployed, but it was possible.

At the time around my fourteen-year mark in service, I was married, the father of three kids, running a small business on the side training bodyguards, teaching aerobics at the local health spa, fighting professionally, training K-9s professionally and for sport competitions, and being a Special Ops soldier. Throw in attending college and you have one over-amped, carbon-based, bi-pedal, sleep-deprived, super human…or a zombie. But I had a mission. I had made a promise to my father and myself—to earn that degree and make him proud.

I love my family, and I, as we all do, have a responsibility to them. Even while in service, I needed to be the best father and husband that I could be. That meant in order for me to give them my best, I had to give them my time. While I went to school, I made it a point to never study or do homework while I was around them. I would wait until everyone was asleep and then get up, go to the kitchen table, and begin my schoolwork. I studied during my lunch breaks, and I brought my books and materials to the field on deployments—I studied every opportunity that presented itself.

I was able to accomplish a lot outside of the military. I earned so many certifications, titles, and achievements that people would ask me how I was able to do so much. My answer was simple: I formulated a plan, managed my time, and made sure there was balance in my life between work and play. Because I enjoyed camping, dancing, traveling, and sports with my kids, I don't feel like I gave up anything—I had fun and I reached my goals.

"Be all that you can be."

That was the Army motto when I enlisted, and it is the mantra I still live by today. It has been the beat that I have always marched to—it was my battle cry while striving for personal victory and the war won't end until I'm dead.

I never did end up making it as a Ranger, though. After I enlisted in the Army, I was told that Ranger school was not an option because the Ranger-school slots were limited.

I was duped by Uncle Sam.

Just like I was promised free health and dental care for life for my family and me when I retired if I accepted less money than I was worth to serve. I retired and did my part, and today I pay for my own health care and dental insurance, but that's a story for a different time.

Death from Above

82ND ABN LRRPs 1984

9

In 1981, I ended up in the 82nd ABN Division (Death from Above) 325th Infantry. At that time, the Army was still going through a post-Vietnam transition. We still wore Vietnam-era jungle camouflage, donned steel pots, and carried M-16 A-1s. Blackhawk helicopters were just being introduced, and drinking two beers during lunch and watching strippers at the post-enlisted club on Fort Bragg were still the norm. In my platoon, with the exception of five people—my high school buddies, and best friends to this day, Joe and Kenny; my platoon SGT, who was a Vietnam vet with the 7th Cavalry; my twenty-two-year-old platoon leader, and me—everyone was a pothead. They would smoke so much that marijuana plants grew at the base of the barracks where the seeds the guys swept off the windowsills would land.

It was a surreal experience. On one hand, there seemed to be a general disregard for order; on the other hand, these guys were some serious badasses who could operate and maneuver like a well-oiled machine in the field.

We used to go to the field for six-week rotations, deploying Monday morning and returning Friday afternoon. We would go to the field and practice movement to contact, immediate actions drills, and fire and maneuver. We'd also dig foxholes to occupy for a few hours, or to sleep in, just to fill them back up.

We operated 24/7 with less than four hours of sleep every day. We carried all of our gear and C-rations (cans of food) in rucksacks that were the size of paper grocery bags. Day in and day out. We would come back Friday, clean our weapons, and then party like rock stars for the weekend. As a platoon, we used to drink beer and raise hell all weekend in the barracks. More often than not, we would beat the crap out of each other, then go back to the field and train to fight as brothers in arms.

My platoon won the Division ARTEP, a field evaluation that compared all of the infantry platoons for combat readiness. I couldn't believe—or maybe I could—that this platoon of beer-drinking, brawlin' dope smokers could kick ass and be the best in a division of 15,000 paratroopers. It was because of this stellar achievement that the division commander, General Lindsey, selected my platoon to be the first Long Range Reconnaissance Platoon (LRRP) since Vietnam. Eventually we were renamed Long Range Surveillance and the concept became an Army-wide capability.

I distinctly remember one cold, frosty morning lying inside of our company defensive perimeter miles out in the woods on Fort Bragg. The sun was starting to rise, and we were all on guard, pulling what's called "stand to" and preparing for a pre-dawn attack by some notional enemy.

As I lay there shivering, thinking about how bad this sucked and peering down my rifle sights, I saw this guy running about twenty-five meters across our perimeter in front of me. He was wearing blue jeans, a T-shirt, jungle boots, and an Army rucksack, and he had long hair and a bushy mustache. I looked over at my foxhole buddy and asked him, "Who in the hell is that?" He told me it was "one of those Delta Force guys." I said, "Delta Force?" Never heard of them. He went on to tell me—as if trying not to divulge too much information because they may somehow know and then something bad would happen to him—that they were this secret unit of handpicked soldiers considered the best in the world. They were America's secret weapon and seeing this guy running through the woods was like spotting Big Foot.

Now I was intrigued. I remember thinking how cool it was that this guy could operate alone, while I was being baby-sat in the woods, not trusted to even take a shit without telling someone where I was going, when I was coming back, who I was going with, what I would do if I got hit while gone, and what I would do if the unit got attacked while I was releasing butt bombs into the bush.

How could I get into a unit like that? I wondered. Could I be good enough? Could I be one of the best soldiers in the world? Only time would tell...

Operation Urgent Fury

Dale Grenada

10

After successfully completing the Delta Force Operator Training Course (OTC), I was assigned "across the hall" to an assault squadron. I remember the first time I reported to the squadron sergeant major (SGM), known as Jack A., who welcomed me and gave me my initial briefing. After introducing himself, he said, "Selection is a continuous process, and just because you are here today, doesn't mean you're guaranteed a job here tomorrow. If you don't put out 110% effort every day, then there is no place for you here." Immediately I "rogered-up" and vowed to meet everyone's expectations every day I was there.

I went on to be assigned to an assault team, with the additional responsibility of being the team breacher. Because of the job, I had to become the subject-matter expert (SME) on ballistic, explosive, mechanical, and manual-entry techniques.

During my time on the team, I put myself through school to become a certified locksmith, and attended courses in surreptitious methods of entry (SMOE) and defense against methods of entry (DAME). I figured the extra skill sets would come in handy if we, or I, needed to enter a target quietly.

As the years went by—a total of nine-and-a-half years in the unit—I had the opportunity to attend many schools and training courses, and I did. I felt it was my responsibility to the Army and my fellow operators to be the best-trained soldier I could be. It was also important that I continue to seek self-improvement so that when I reached retirement, assuming I was not killed first, I would be prepared to continue to support my family and be a productive and contributing member of our country.

I attended the Special Forces Qualification Course (SFQC) while assigned to the Delta Force—known as the Unit. At only twenty-three years old, I was one of the youngest guys ever assigned to the Unit and had very little formal training. Most operators were former Rangers, Green Berets, or both. I was neither. I was an airborne infantryman and a long-range scout. Besides basic infantry training and jump school, I gathered all of my training in-house in the 82nd Airborne Division.

My first combat experience was with the LRS platoon in the small Caribbean island of Grenada, where we had conducted static surveillance from the surrounding isles to interdict the People's Revolutionary Army of Grenada (PRA) and the Cubans who were holding out and staging from the isles, recovering weapons caches.

When Operation Urgent Fury into Grenada went down, I was in Recondo School at Fort Bragg. I remember we were up at 5:00 AM and in PT formation. On this particular day, the Bragg and the Pope Air Force Base thrummed with activity. Fighter jets traced through the air with C-130s and C-141s, landing as fast as they could right behind each other.

We had no idea what was going on until the cadre called us out of formation, telling us to report back to our units. By the time I got back to my platoon, they had already staged their equipment and were on their way to Green Ramp, an area on Pope AFB where we would assemble and load aircraft to conduct parachute operations. Since I was late getting back, I was told I would catch a follow-on bird and escort communications and other supplies to Grenada before linking up with my platoon. It sounded reasonable and simple.

Turns out it was not simple, and it became very unreasonable the minute I set foot on the island.

I flew to Grenada on a C-141. Only a handful of us occupied the bird. I had a few crates of radios and other supplies with me. The aircraft arrived late in the afternoon in Point Salines and taxied to a makeshift airfield operations center, which was mainly a small tent with sand bags and radio antennas. Because of the potential threat to the aircraft, the planes only landed and took off during daylight hours. They would conduct a hot offload and immediately take off to avoid being sitting targets.

With a little help, I was able to off-load all the gear and move it from the tarmac quickly. The plane took off without delay, as did the others who had been on the bird with me. As I looked around for the guys meeting me to pick up the gear and take me to camp, it soon became obvious that they weren't there and were probably not coming for me.

A first lieutenant, who was acting as the airfield commanding officer (AFO), told me I couldn't stay there. I asked him if he knew where or how I could reach my unit, but he had no idea and no tolerance to discuss the issue and work out a solution. He simply ordered me to leave.

It was dark; I was a young Specialist 4th Class (SPEC-4), and I was utterly lost as to what to do or where to go.

I decided to start walking, because this prick had made it clear he was not going to help me. He was gracious enough to give me some ammunition and a box of C-rations before I ventured off into the valley of death. Unsure of where to go, I started heading north. Remember, bad guys were running around, and the good guys were willing to shoot anyone with a weapon outside of their perimeter at night. The whole situation was insane. I kept thinking that I shouldn't be walking around in a combat zone by myself at night with no idea of my destination.

I walked until I reached Saint Georges, the capital of Grenada. I wasn't too comfortable with the location, so I turned around and walked southeast along a coastal road. It was dark, and heavy jungle vegetation lined both sides of the road. Without warning, an American voice came out of the darkness. I heard, "Halt, who goes there?"

At once, I recognized the voice of one of my LRS teammates. It was a relief to meet him in total darkness and know I was safe. We jumped around like giddy schoolgirls since I was an unexpected surprise for him too. Apparently, my unit had not been informed that I was on my way.

That night, after I successfully hooked up with my LRRP team, I slept in the grass at what was formerly the US Embassy, and the next day we sent teams out to the isles, leaving them there for days to observe and interdict enemy forces approaching.

The previous week, on Green Isle (a small island about two miles off Grenada, approximately 300 x 300 meters in size), one of our LRRP teams had a chance contact with PRA militia who were recovering a weapons cache on the beach.

Two of the five LRRP team members were wounded in a firefight with approximately five enemies. The PRA's left-side security position ambushed them, opening up on the patrol at point-blank range.

Two of the men, Kurt and Stephen, returned fire, though wounded, and managed to roll under a wooden shack on the beach. The PRA fired Soviet tracers into the shack and it caught fire on top of Kurt and Stephen. The LRRPs returned effective fire and knocked down several of the adversaries. Those capable pulled their wounded into a small boat and sped off.

The Quick Reaction Force (QRF) that was supposed to be on strip alert with a reaction time of less than twenty minutes did not arrive until the next day—about twelve hours late. On the way to Green Isle by helicopter, they recovered two floaters in the ocean who had died from gunshot wounds and hand-grenade fragmentation. Despite this delay, Stephen and Kurt survived to have several other adventures, making them the two most decorated soldiers of Operation Urgent Fury.

Stephen and Kurt were awarded Silver Stars, Purple Hearts, and soldiers' metals for rescuing a Grenadian boy who was drowning when his fishing boat overturned. Unfortunately, of the three boys in the boat, only one was rescued. The boys were spotted when a team was on their way back from a mission. Kurt rappelled from his helicopter and grabbed the drowning boy from the water. As the helicopter lifted the boy and Kurt out of the water, everyone watching was amazed to see the kid holding on to a small shark he had caught and did not want to part with.

I was pulling security late one night on the same island when I heard a Cobra helicopter circling the island. He changed his vector and was headed directly for us. I could hear the whopping of the blades as he went into a dive and then leveled off.

A moment later, he fired a flare directly overhead then vectored into a right-hand bank. At this point, my five-man LRRP team was awake and on the radio, trying to reach the bird to no avail. It only took us seconds to realize he was using the island for target practice. Before we could react, he began strafing the island with a 20 mm chain gun and rockets. He made his first pass, and then circled for a re-attack. By this time, we were running to the edge of the island where we stopped before a one-hundred-foot drop into the rocky ocean below. We all reached into our load-bearing equipment, pulled out our emergency strobe lights, and shone them around us in a 360-degree pattern. As the pilot was nose down on his gun-run, he saw the strobes and disengaged.

The next morning, we got a situation report (SITREP) and were extracted back to base.

Selection—
A Continuous Process

Delta Selection Cadre

11

I reached the end of my first four years of enlistment and had to make a decision. Do I stay or do I get out? I was twenty-two with my first wife and first daughter, Danielle, who was a year old. I had no skills or education that would help me in the civilian world, or at least that's what I thought. Ironically, I received a recruitment letter from the Delta Force, the Unit, telling me that I met all of the prerequisites to come to their recruitment briefing. I decided that as much as I loved the 82nd and seeing it grow into a modern professional Army, which had eliminated pot and fun stuff like strippers, beer for lunch, and yelling obscenities at other units while running down the streets during physical fitness training, that it was time to move on to a new stage in my life. I needed more and I knew I could do more. I needed to be all that I could be. Therefore, I reenlisted with one goal in mind—to be a Delta operator.

I went to all of the pre-briefings and evaluations, background checks, physical examinations, psyche evaluations, and physical fitness tests, which I passed all of. I was chosen to attend the selection and assessment course in the fall. At the same time, I came down on orders to prepare for a permanent assignment at Fort Polk, Louisiana, within a week of completing the S&A course.

I was in big trouble, because I had bought a small house and I was in no way prepared to move to Fort Polk. Fort Polk was the last place that I wanted to be assigned. It was like being relegated to a swamp away from civilization. I decided that failing the Unit S&A was not an option; therefore, I didn't make any preparations for an impending assignment to Fort Polk. This was a dangerous but gutsy move on my part because, had I failed selection, I would have seriously disrupted my family's life and mine.

The Unit selection course is by far one of the toughest selection courses of any service. Unlike other training and selection courses, like the SEALs' BUD/S training, the Special Forces Qualification Course to be a Green Beret, and Army Ranger School, where teamwork is the medium for success or failure, Delta selection is an individual effort. Soldiers are given very limited but specific instructions to perform for days on end in austere conditions. The physiological challenge, the isolation, wears down their will to win. The psychological and emotional head games that they play are theirs alone, manifested from their own fears and doubts. The attrition rate is the highest in the military, and the chances of success are unlikely for even the most physically and mentally adept.

But, I'll be damned—I made it! When the dust settled, less than three percent of my starting class remained and I wasn't going to Fort Polk.

My tenure in Delta Force was one of the greatest experiences of my life. It wasn't a job—it was a commitment to a way of life that had me looking forward to the day's adventure, and to returning home, knowing that every day I accomplished something that made me a better soldier, the organization a better Unit, and America safer.

Top Gun

Me and My Tactical .45, Training Portuguese SEALs in
Combat Marksmanship

12

When I was twenty-two going through OTC, I experienced another moment in my life that was as humiliating and disconcerting as the one when I was a teenager playing baseball for the Pattonville Royals.

The OTC, which prepares the candidate for his assignment to a squadron, lasted six months. It covered a range of topics and skills, including advanced combat marksmanship, close-quarter battle, and medical, plus many other skills that cannot be learned in the conventional Army, nor that a soldier would be expected to learn.

Unfortunately, these skill sets fall into the classified realm because of their nature and nexus with the Unit. It suffices to say that the training offers everything the ultimate soldier would need to know to carry out any mission, whether in a unit or as a single operator.

Delta Force operators are considered the best combat marksmen in the world. We have beaten every counter-terrorism force worldwide, including the SEALs. In fact, many of today's marksmanship techniques derive from the Unit operators. We have mastered the art of weapon craft with the same commitment black belts have to martial arts.

Because surgical shooting was our stock in trade, we trained long and hard. We could not afford to be mediocre shots or have clumsy fingers when handling firearms. Civilians, non-combatants, and our fellow soldiers could not, and should not, become victims of lousy training or incompetent operators.

In the beginning of OTC, we trained for weeks, eight to ten hours a day, practicing dry-fire techniques that systematically taught us the target identification to target acquisition cycle. We rehearsed drawing the weapon from the holster, mounting a sub-gun or carbine into the shoulder, and executing multiple trigger presses and recovery drills ad nauseam. When I went home to sleep at night, my dreams only consisted of the four-point draw, up-drills, tactical, admin, and combat reloads. I don't know how I ever got any rest.

The lead instructor was a Vietnam vet, very short and with a big mustache, who reminded me of Yosemite Sam.

Mr. Yosemite Sam was an interesting character. He was a good man whose only interest was training us to be the best operators possible. He wanted to ensure every man who passed OTC was indeed the right man, worthy of a walk across the hall to an assault squadron. However, as well intentioned as his heart was, he was an abrasive fellow with the personality of a bobcat trapped in a phone booth.

During about the third week of dry-fire training (training with no live ammo) in the classroom, Yosemite Sam called the class to a halt in the middle of the session—this was a pivotal day for me. He duly pointed out—in front of everyone—that my form was sloppy and inconsistent.

I thought I was at least on par with the average guys in the class, so the tongue-lashing I received that day caught me off guard. Yosemite went so far as to pull out the video camera and publicly show me how jacked up I was. He told me in front of my peers that if I did not make an immediate and significant improvement, I wouldn't make it.

The funny thing was, by the end of the lashing, I still didn't know what in the hell he was talking about. One thing was for sure—he was gunning for me. I knew I had to impress the hell out of him fast, or else I was going to do the duffle-bag drag to the front gate and have to look for a new job.

That evening at home, I by-passed dinner, walked by my wife and kids, and made my way to the bedroom. I told my wife not to disturb me, as I was going to bed because I needed to practice firearms training. Though she had no idea what that meant, she knew by my tone that it was serious, and it was best to leave me alone.

I was in a desperate situation. I had not come this far to wash out. It would be an epic tragedy that my pride would not let me cope with, and would probably wound my ego for life. I knew I had to reach down deep and muster all of my experience and willpower to overcome this problem. The only thing that gave me confidence and peace of mind was my experience as a kid when I inadvertently learned the concept of autogenic conditioning. Since it had worked for me before and I somewhat understood the concept, I went back into that mode of deep meditation and visualization.

I turned on some enjoyable music, lay in bed, and closed my eyes. I visualized every step in the four-point draw.

The cycle consisted of exact movements whereby I grasped the pistol and released the holster thumb snap simultaneously. My purchase of the pistol grip had to be perfect. It had to be high on the beaver tail with the trigger finger elongated on the outside of the holster in line with the trigger guard. As I drew the weapon and the muzzle cleared the top of the holster, I had to cant the weapon forward with the muzzle pointed in the direction of the threat. As I raised the weapon to the center of my chest, my non-firing hand met and grasped my firing hand. As I secured the weapon with two hands, I extended the weapon at eye level, focusing on the front sight and centering both sites on the target. At the end of the extension, I pressed the trigger, reset the sear, and was prepared to press the trigger again. As I finished servicing the target, I retraced the lines of weapon presentation back to the holster.

This may not sound too complicated, but I left out about two hundred sub-tasks—administrative, tactical, and combat reload drills, malfunction drills, off-hand shooting, and enough else to fill a separate book.

It was critical that I know exactly how every technique should look and feel. Otherwise, I would have been practicing the technique incorrectly and permanently burned the errors into my long-term memory.

Hence, as I visualized the techniques, I broke them down into small chunks in my mind. Once I mastered a small portion, I practiced the next portion. Once I mastered two portions, I chained them together. Once I mastered a series of two, I visualized a third portion until I mastered it. I then added it to the chain and created a series of three portions that flowed together seamlessly into one. I continued this process until I mastered all the modules alone and as part of the sequence. I performed this mental rehearsal for about six hours until I could see and feel every movement as if I were actually performing the task.

The next day I went back to training with renewed confidence. I knew that what I did the previous night equaled three weeks' worth of training. As the day proceeded, I followed the instructions and executed the tasks the way that I knew how.

The first day went by without critique.

The second day went by and I still had no indication of how well I was doing. One could surmise that this was the calm before the storm. In fact, I always say that as long as your boss or mentor, or wife, is yelling at you, then they still think you have potential. When they get quiet—it's all over but the crying.

At the end of day three, Yosemite Sam gathered us into the classroom for a hot wash. A hot wash is an after-action review (AAR) or critique. As we all sat and waited in anticipation, I remember thinking, "Is this going to be my swan song?"

Sam walked to the center of the group and asked me to stand up. A sense of foreboding came over me as I braced for impact.

Sam asked the students to take a good look at me. Then, in front of all, he declared me the most fundamentally sound student in the class and predicted that I would win the Top Gun Award at the end of the course. Amazed at how much I had improved in three days, he never again criticized me.

I became amazingly proficient with tactical .45 pistols. I could shoot with remarkable speed, accuracy, and safety. My movements became fluid, instinctive, and efficient. On the last day of our small-arms marksmanship training, we had to undergo an evaluation. The test was called Man-on-Man Shoot Out, and it was for the title of Top Gun.

Two students would stand on a firing line, facing an array of steel targets placed in various configurations. Some were sheets of metal half the size of a man, others were steel plates, and some were steel sheets shaped like bowling pins. Each shooter's targets were set up at the same distance and in the same order. They were set to fall over if shot, indicating that they had been successfully engaged.

The last target was a dueling tree—one vertical pole with two steel flags on each side that swing, when hit, to the other side of the pole. This was the last target both shooters could engage. The shooter could not proceed to the next target until having successfully knocked over the previous one.

Once at the dueling tree, especially if it was a close match, we could increase our opponent's flag count by one if we hit our flags.

At this point, the shootout could be intense, because we were engaging 3 x 3 inch flags at about ten meters, and it was a race to hit both of our flags and swing them to the opponent's side.

It finally came down to me and one other student—we were the two best shooters in the class.

The race was on.

Our targets were dropping as fast as we could acquire them and press our triggers. As I got to my second-to-last target, a standing half-sized silhouette of a man, I was ahead of my opponent by at least one target. I hit the target and moved on to the dueling tree. I noticed out of my peripheral vision that my last target was wobbling but had not yet fallen. Its stand hadn't been balanced properly. Afraid to break the rules and engage a target before the previous one fell, I traversed back to reengage it.

As soon as I came off the tree, the silhouette fell and now my opponent was on the tree before me. As I came back on target, he hit his first flag and then I hit mine. As quickly as possible, I tried to get my second flag before he got his.

Time seemed to slow down. I pressed my trigger as he pressed his and to my surprise, and everyone else's, his flag swung around a microsecond before mine…

I had lost the duel.

I walked away with my head held high, because I knew, as did everyone, the one target that wobbled was out of my control. I was still happy that I came in second, and in my heart and mind, I was the undeclared champion for having risen from the bottom to the top.

Lone Operator

Lone Operator

13

An operator is selected because he has inherent traits and characteristics that make him versatile enough so that he can operate alone, as a team unilaterally, or as part of a task force that consists of other military assets jointly working toward a common objective. Delta operators are physically fit, mature, and trustworthy professionals. They are men who can do anything they are tasked with, whether it be to field an artillery team, fly an aircraft, jump from an airplane at 30,000 feet at night with an oxygen tank and combat equipment, or kill a grizzly bear with a spear—whatever the mission calls for. They can do anything and will train until they are the best at the task.

Killing a grizzly bear with a spear was not something I looked forward to; I would have preferred a buck knife so that I could get close and whisper in his ears as I turned his lights out, "Sleep tight, my little teddy bear." But I still carried out the task. Okay, we didn't kill grizzly bears…but we would have assuming we were adequately drunk.

Who are these men? We are not average men, although many of us look like the guy next door, mowing grass and getting bitched out by the wife because we haven't taken the trash out yet.

We all are not necessarily these super athletic-looking guys that we often see in the movies. What makes us larger than life are our hearts, our minds, our belief in the American way of life, and our dedication to preserving it. Operators tend to be predominately conservative, religious men that put God, country, and family first. We are the sheep dogs that stand vigil over America and are prepared to fight the wolf should he come to prey upon the flock. We are motivated by the glory of combat; we are not afraid to fight and eagerly go to battle because we are empowered by righteousness, courage, training, and honor.

Men like this are so rare that some selection processes have yielded only one candidate. These are the men the rest of the military tries to model themselves after. They are tier-one, and in the hierarchy of military society, they are on the pinnacle, followed by SEAL Team Six, Green Berets, Rangers, 82nd LRS, and Marine Force Recon. This comparison usually doesn't sit well with members of the other services or units, but someone with special insight who can make the distinctions in assessment, selection, training, and mission will show you the disparity.

Then again, I don't want to take anything away from the rest of the military or its service members. The fact is that we are all one team and we are here to fight the same fight. Every unit, like every soldier, Marine, sailor, or airman, has certain responsibilities to carry out. Some tasks are more difficult than others and require certain capabilities and knowhow. But the reality is, by virtue of its mission, the Unit has elevated its capabilities in manpower, equipment, specialized training, and logistics to a level that is unrivaled in any modern military.

The first retort that I always hear from naysayers is that "Delta doesn't dive, whereas the SEALs do." Let me just say here again, the Unit can do anything. The credo of the Special Forces, which Delta is a kindred spirit of, states, "By land, by sea, by air." Army Special Forces, Rangers, LRSU, and Special Ops have a dive capability—diving is not solely the domain of the Navy.

I ended up spending twenty-nine years in the military and working for the government as a contract intelligence officer. I also had received training in operations and intelligence while I was a Green Beret. This skill set would allow me to conduct intelligence analyses of the enemy, friendly forces, and battle space, and to anticipate enemy courses of action, all in the effort to aid in the development of our battle strategy.

My training also taught me the use of tradecraft to conduct low visibility ops, often alone, in support of military and government-sanctioned operations. The military and government agencies routinely have exchange programs so that specialized capabilities can be shared. This sharing of capabilities, knowledge, and skills enhances the overall capabilities of the American military and intelligence community.

Special Forces—
The Green Berets

My Green Beret A-Team, Kuwait 1999

14

To earn the military occupational skills designator of 18 Bravo (18B), I attended the Special Forces Qualification Course to become a light-and-heavy weapons expert. With this training, I was now a Green Beret with the responsibility of overseeing anything from employment of weapons and security to base defense and combat operations. I would be the subject-matter expert on an A-Team, with expertise in training and combat operations, including direct actions missions (DA), strategic reconnaissance (SR), counter-terrorism (CT), unconventional warfare (UW), and foreign internal defense (FID).

This course was exceptionally difficult for me because I was going through a divorce, which my wife at the time had notified me of about two weeks after I started. To make matters worse, she moved out and left me with my eighteen-month-old son. I got up every morning at 0430 hours, found a baby sitter, went to school all day, and arrived home at around 1800 hours. I would then pick him up, feed him, and prep him for bed. Somewhere in this time, I had to study and get myself ready for the next day too.

Because of not eating and a lack of sleep, I lost seventeen pounds in three weeks. The cadre, who was aware of my situation and concerned that I would not be fit enough to complete training, told me if I did not maintain my weight, they were going to put me on a military meal card and insist I eat my rations at school.

The course lasted six months. Every morning we formed up for our daily physical fitness training. It usually consisted of a multi-mile run led by Sergeant First Class Gola, who could run like a cheetah. SFC Gola's mission was to run so fast for so long that we would all fall out. Then he would come back and exercise us to death as punishment.

Thankfully, I was relatively lean and a fast runner, so I never fell out, though, I felt like it more than once. Some mornings we conducted a long rucksack march to prepare us for the twelve-mile rucksack march at the end of the first phase. It would be a timed event. The standard time for a twelve-mile ruck march on flat terrain—with a forty-pound backpack, a weapon, load-bearing equipment, and two quarts of water—was three hours or less. I had completed an eighteen-mile ruck march at night through mountainous terrain with the same equipment standards.

At this point in my life, my ex-wife and I were in and out of our relationship. It was a tumultuous time for me, but I couldn't drop out of the Q Course. It was a matter of pride. I had legitimate cause to go back to the unit and try to regroup, and then come back to the Q Course when my personal problems were resolved. However, I decided I was stronger than that and that I would hang in there and earn my Special Forces' tab like everyone else. I was not going to quit.

The day of the twelve-mile ruck march finally arrived. It was to be held on a Friday night, starting at 2000 hours on Tank Trail Road at Fort Bragg. This road was deep beach sand and thus very difficult to walk in.

Earlier that day, my company first sergeant had noticed I was out of sorts. To be honest, I was beleaguered with my personal struggles and my enthusiasm to hang in there was starting to wane. He didn't want me to do the road march; he knew I had things on my mind that I needed to take care of. Several times in the past I had completed a six-event physical fitness test comprised of push-ups, sit-ups, a two-mile run with combat boots, run-dodge-jump, an inverted crawl, and a one hundred meter swim followed by an eighteen mile ruck march. I completed the course in two hours, fifty-seven minutes, which was faster than anyone else. I had also once completed a forty-mile trek with the Unit in rain and snow in fifteen hours and thirty-six minutes, so he knew a twelve-mile march was like a walk in the park for me.

I took my first sergeant's advice and went home. Once I was home, it was no surprise that my wife and I began to fight. I left the house and went to the local bar to have a beer and decompress.

I have never been much of a drinker, and during that time, I did not drink at all. I am not sure why I went there; maybe I was hoping to see someone I knew who could help put a smile back on my face. After my eighth beer, I was feeling very drunk and in no condition to do anything. As I peered across the room, I saw my first sergeant sitting at the bar talking with some friends. He looked over and acknowledged me with a toast. He had given me the night off to take care of personal issues, and here I was, drunk. The guilt I felt was overwhelming. My cohorts were getting ready to hump their asses off under rucks, and I was about to have another beer! I looked at my watch and realized they would begin in an hour. In that span I knew I could get home, change into my uniform, grab my ruck and kit, and get a ride to Bragg in time to make the march, so that's exactly what I did, while staggering drunk.

The march down the dirt road was like walking in a funnel. The forest on the side of the road created a dark wall, while the white sand on the road guided my path. Above was a gray star-lit sky that seemed like something out of a nightmare. I remember looking up and seeing the sky spin. Dehydration from the alcohol caused the psychedelic effects I was experiencing. I honestly did not know whether the march was really happening or whether I was going to wake up in my bed and realize it was all a dream, but I drunkenly completed the ruck march, finishing last at two hours and fifty-nine minutes!

I successfully completed the Q Course and returned to my unit in December 1989. The day after returning, I went out with my troop to conduct close-quarter battle training for an impending mission into Panama.

That day, as luck would have it, I received a fragmentation wound from a stun grenade. I know that sounds like an oxymoron—a stun grenade that throws fragmentation—but it happened.

I had been the number one man in a stack, or an assault line-up, and we were preparing to enter a room to clear it of any threats. I pulled the door open so my number two man could throw a stun grenade into the room. He threw the grenade without looking, and it bounced back and detonated next to my left heel. Back then, the stun grenades, or flash bangs as they're commonly called, were first generation and packed one hell of a wallop.

When the banger went off, it launched two pieces of cardboard (1 x .25 x 3 inches each) into my left calf muscle. Metal and wood shavings entered my wound too. The blast blew my leg out from under me. I landed on my back, bleeding profusely.

I walked away with a five-inch vertical scar on my leg that I still carry today. I was relegated to crutches and temporary staff duty until I healed and could train again. On staff duty, I had to sit in an office over night, answer phones, and be the watchman for the entire unit and its property.

On December 17, 1989, I received a phone call on the Redline from the Joint Special Operations Command (JSOC). After I confirmed its owner's identity, the voice said the following words to me: "Alert your unit, Operation Acid Gambit is in effect. N-Hour is 2100 hours, confirm receipt."

I sprang into action and paged the alert squadron, which happened to be mine, summoning them to the unit. I sent out the classified pager codes, notifying everyone that needed to know that this was not a drill.

Carcel Modelo

On our way to Modelo Prison, December 20, 1989

"War is an extension of politics, and the Soldier
is the last few feet of diplomacy." —Dale Comstock

15

The first operators arrived within twenty minutes. Shortly thereafter, my troop commander arrived and came by the staff duty office. At this point, it was organized chaos. I filled him in on the details and he asked a few questions. The last thing he said before he left the office was: "Dale, I know you're injured and you're having marital problems, but this mission is like the Super Bowl for us and you are a key player. I wouldn't feel right not giving you the opportunity to come with us if that's what you want. But, I wouldn't blame you if you stayed behind. Your call…"

I was the senior breacher in the troop and I was part of the team. I didn't have to think long and hard on this one. I was ecstatic he had even considered me and I gleefully agreed to go. I stripped off my suit and tie and put on my flight suit and assault boots. Within a few hours, I was on my way to Panama to become a part of what is considered the first successful hostage rescue mission in US military history.

16

On December 20, 1989, I found myself at Howard Air Force Base in Panama. My team and I were conducting final preparations for the impending mission that night. Modelo Prison was in downtown Panama, across from the *Comandancia*—Manuel Noriega's headquarters. Our mission was to breach it and rescue Kurt Muse, who was being held captive for spying on the Panamanian government. According to records, Kurt was an American businessman working in Panama City. He was also a member of the local Rotary Club, which is how his trouble started. He was arrested by the Panamanian government for collecting signal intelligence (SIGINT) for the US government. Basically, Kurt was allegedly electronically intercepting the Panamanian government's military communications. This allegation has never been confirmed.

Other incidents involving the US military and their dependents led up to the decision by the United States to remove Noriega from power with military action. Our part was to spearhead the invasion by launching a raid on Modelo Prison. We would rescue Kurt, and then the rest of the US military would come into Panama within minutes to secure the country.

After our final briefings and rehearsals, I went to the troop medic to have the staples removed from my injured leg, and have my calf bandaged securely. I had injured myself not long before during a training accident—I'd received some shrapnel from a flashbang, and damn did it cause some damage. I had needed staples, and wasn't sure if I'd be able to go on this op. Thing is, I wasn't about to pass it up, so I bandaged myself up, and decided I'd go. This way I could function and not worry about my leg during the raid.

Seven hours before the raid, we were notified that operational security had been broken by at least two American servicemen in-country. A Marine private had called home to his parents (via landline) to tell them he loved them, that something was going to happen, and that he may never see them again. An Army military policeman (MP) told a local family he was friends with to stay away from the canal, the Bridge of the Americas, and downtown Panama City. He told them the US military was going to carry out a secret operation.

Of course, these two incidents alerted Noriega's Panamanian Defense Force (PDF) and the local militia, the Dignitary Battalion (DIGBAT). DIGBAT was an organized and armed group of civilians that augmented the PDF. Since it only made sense to hit the headquarters, both groups knew there would be an attack on the *Comandancia*. And since Kurt Muse was there, they were aware that Modelo Prison was also a potential target.

We delayed the on target hit time (H-Hour) by about twenty minutes. The decision was made to execute after midnight, regardless of the enemy situation. Because the PDF was expecting an attack, they started reinforcing the anticipated targets.

Our snipers/observers were already in the jungle on the edges of the city, watching the Modelo and the *Comandancia*. They reported .50 caliber machine-gun emplacements were being installed on all of the street corners, either vehicle mounted or sandbagged on rooftop corners, as more soldiers were filling the area and establishing defensive fighting positions. Modelo Prison normally had about sixty guards on staff at any one time. Now it was reinforced with PDF soldiers, raising their numbers to about one-hundred-twenty shooters.

Because of all the activity, the locals started to gather on the streets around the targets. They came out in the hundreds with lawn chairs and music. Many drove and parked their cars and just stayed and waited for what they thought, and what I would imagine if I were them, was going to be something like the Rose Bowl Parade.

Before we knew it, the streets and sidewalks were full of adults and kids just hanging out. This situation created a problem for everyone. When you have innocent kids and adults in and around a target where lead is going to fly, lighting is scant, and bad guys are prowling...there's going to be drama.

17

We loaded the birds at Howard AFB and rendered a head count to verify everyone was aboard and ready to fight. I remember one of my teammates asked me to switch weapons with him as we loaded the bird.

I carried a CAR-15 with an M-203 grenade launcher and an Aimpoint 2000. He carried a CAR-15 without the grenade launcher. I was going into the target to rescue Muse, while he would stay on the roof in a support position, engaging the guard towers and ground forces.

Because we used Aimpoints, the weapons were zeroed to the adjunct sights and not to the shooter. That means anyone could have picked up any weapon and hit their targets as accurately as the owner. I agreed to switch, since it made sense that the enemy would be better served with 40 mm grenades off the rooftop. I didn't want to cheat the enemy out of the full experience that they were due.

We had an excess of twelve helicopters, including gunships. I was on one of four MH-6 Little Birds, a very versatile bird. MH-6s are equipped with "people pods" on their outsides; these are basically benches that seat two operators on each side. These small and fast helicopters allow for landings in constricted areas. What is more amazing is that the first generation engines were used for irrigation and now they're used to keep men and machines aloft.

The mission was to land all four birds on the roof of the three-story-high Modelo Prison. The birds would land two by two. I was on the left people pod of the first bird with the main breaching charge. My assistant team leader (ATL) was sitting next to me with a Broco torch wrapped in Kevlar.

The tank on his back was full of pure oxygen and would probably blow up if struck by a bullet or exposed to any spark. I remember the discomfort I had when I put my seating arrangement in perspective: I was carrying several pounds of high explosives, sitting next to a guy with a scuba tank of pure oxygen on his back, while we both sat on the pods of an alloy helicopter filled with jet fuel, which was going to fly us into a hail of bullets, brimstone, and fire. Man, what was I thinking when I told SSG Dobbins at the recruiting office to put away the brochures on cushy electronics jobs and make me a barrel-chested Ranger!

The birds lifted off for a one-minute-and-forty-six-second flight to target. All we had to do was cross on the west side of the Bridge of the Americas over the Panama Canal and then through the saddle of Ancon Hill, straight into Modelo.

As we flew low and slow through the saddle, we heard shooting from our snipers below. They were stacking up bad guys like cordwood.

As we approached at forty-five feet off the deck, at what seemed to be about thirty miles an hour, it was quite evident to the civilians that no Rose Bowl Parade was coming tonight. They scrambled, screaming and clutching their children. They scattered in every direction like cockroaches in a dirty kitchen when the lights come on. Between the civilians, PDF, and DIGBAT, it was difficult to target-discriminate, though we were taking a lot of rounds from the ground from the enemy interspersed among the civilians.

18

I remember my first confirmed kill like it happened just a moment ago. My bird was hovering over the prison and sinking to land on the roof next to the 10 x 10 annex I would have to breach to get us into the prison. As the bird hovered, I saw a group of five women, two holding children, run across the street from the prison entrance to a cemetery opening. They were no more than twenty-five meters from my sight. I suddenly realized in the middle of the cluster of women was a DIGBAT member carrying an AK-47 (with folding stock). He carried it at port arms with the muzzle aimed at my bird. He wore a white guayabera shirt and blue jeans and was about thirty-five years old.

At this point, I was prepared to shoot and leveled my weapon at him. However, I decided to wait for two reasons. First, the helicopter was sinking and thus my muzzle was not steady. Second, the women and kids were bobbing around him at shoulder-to-shoulder proximity. They, in effect, were shielding him.

I was concerned, though it was an easy shot, even at night, that I would hit a kid or a woman. I waited another second or two. Anticipating for them to run through the entrance of the cemetery, I hoped they would break left and that he would break off to the right. Thankfully, I was correct.

The cemetery wall was only about four feet tall, and as soon as he turned right, he popped up over the wall. He was leading with his weapon to engage us. Because my spider senses told me he would do that, I was already waiting for him. I pressed the trigger four times and sent my regards his way. He went down behind the wall and never got back up. Goodbye, my friend!

The Little Bird touched down on the roof, and I unsnapped my safety line from its anchor point and proceeded to the breach point. I began the process of placing my explosive charge while the rest of the assault element was still landing and lining up on the side and back of the 10 x 10 foot annex. At this point, the volume of gunfire and explosions was exponentially higher than in the thirty seconds before we reached the building. At the same time, all of the lights and power in the city had gone out.

Guards from the towers, and from the sleeping quarters and the barber shop twenty-five meters away, were cutting loose on us with their blasters. I had bullets zinging by my head and smacking off the wall in front of me. These guys were definitely dialing in on my brain-housing group. Either that or they didn't like my helmet. I assessed the door before I placed the charge and realized, to my surprise, the door configuration was not laid out the way the Agency had described it to me. They said it was a single, standalone steel door in a steel frame attached to cinderblock walls. What I was looking at was a steel door, but with a barred jail door about six inches in front of it.

So I had a standoff between the main door and the outer jail door, and I had limited charge to surface contact on the jail door. In essence, I was going to lose a lot of explosive energy where the charge did not have surface contact.

The charge I assembled for the target door was a rigid-linear charge. All of my explosives would make contact with the door and have enough energy to push it out of its frame. As I built the charge, I calculated the exact amount of explosives required to breach that particular door, which was a fair amount. I thought about the mission, deciding that there would be no friendlies behind the door or on the next level that I needed to concern myself with not injuring. Instead I suspected there would be bad guys on the other side waiting for me, or shooting through the door at me as soon as they realized my position. So, I decided to add the "P" factor. ("P" stands for "Plenty," as in plenty of explosives.) I needed to ensure a positive breach because any delay could cost Kurt his life. I doubled the amount of fairy dust and created a charge that was essentially over-kill to guarantee we would crash the party with a positive entry and no invitation needed.

I adhered the primary charge on the horizontal bars of the jail door as best I could under the conditions. I knew I had plenty of demo to knock the bejesus out of both doors and effect entry. I attached my firing system to the bottom tail of the explosives and attempted to remove the safety cotter pins. Now the tail on the charge was about eight inches long. When I attached the priming system, I added at least another twelve inches and now had about twenty inches of loose detonation cord and firing systems just waiting to grab hold of something and create havoc.

The night was hot, humid, dark, and full of noise as the last operators fell into the stack. As I waited for the signal over the radio, which I could barely hear over the gunfire, I pulled the firing system safeties and grabbed the pull rings on the fuse igniters.

While I sat out in the open in front of the annex door, exposed to the courtyard where the PDF and guards were engaging us, it seemed like an eternity before I got the countdown to breach. I kept expecting bullets to come through the door—though I would have just called that a compromised assault and blasted the doors into the bad guy's face—but that never happened, and then the countdown was coming over the radio, and I was starting the initiation sequence.

Now, without compromising trade secrets, I will say that I pulled the hell out of those firing systems, which were on a ten-second delay.

Because it was dark, I wore standard-issue flight gloves, and with all of the noise and smoke, I wasn't sure if my systems had fired and the time fuse was burning. I contemplated this conundrum, expending at least four or five seconds analyzing the situation. This meant I had about five seconds left to get up and on the other side of the annex before this charge went nuclear and sent me into orbit in pieces and parts.

I jumped and began running. The excessive long tail on my priming system, conveniently, and with malicious intent, grabbed my assault boot and decided the entire ensemble was coming with me. Out of my peripheral vision, I saw the charge come off the door. It looked like a small tree slowly falling over, and I almost think I imagined the word "Timberrrr."

Plop! The damn thing landed behind me and in front of the assault team. I stopped immediately and turned to see this horrific scene. My troop commander yelled to my team leader, "Fix it, Stephen, fix it!" I remember thinking, "What the hell is Stephen going to do? He's in charge but I'm the guy turning wrenches here. Get the fuck outta my way!"

By this time, I had counted the seconds in my head and knew we were safe. The charge had not armed. I ran back into the hail of little gray matter bits—bullets—and grabbed the charge. I returned to the door, took a deep breath, and told myself, "By the numbers, Dale, by the numbers."

I reattached the charge securely, removed all safeties, and then pulled each ring on the igniters. When I pulled the first one, it felt like it didn't fire. In fact, the ring didn't even release the firing pin. So, I moved on to the second ring and pulled. This time it was nice and smooth, and I could feel the firing pin hit the primer and pop. The charge was burning, and we were going into a devil's lair to dance with Santa Muerte.

In my excitement I yelled, "Fire in the hole!" I ran around the side of the annex, which was exposed to enemy gunfire, and jumped into the stack. Kaboom! A beast of a charge shot both doors across to the far side of the wall like flying platters. They hit the wall flush and then slid down the wall. They landed perfectly, resting out of our pathway down the stairs.

The shockwave was incredible. Kurt Muse, who was two floors down in a small jail cell, later described the experience, saying that the overpressure blew the hair on his head back. I can just imagine what the guards were thinking when this shockwave bounced off the walls throughout the building, notifying them that it was game time.

19

We entered the pitch-black building and descended the stairs, starting into hallways and rooms. One poor guard ran out into the hallway and just fell to the floor, surrendering. We threw a couple of flash bangers his way to remind him that, if he moved, we would let the air out of him. He didn't move other than to piss all over himself.

Intelligence had said the guard/interrogator watching Muse was to kill him immediately if anything happened. As one of our assault teams entered the room Muse was being held in, the interrogator ran into a bathroom and stood in the shower with a pistol raised. He was ready to shoot the first operator to follow him. Only a few seconds behind, James, a good friend of mine who I loved like a brother, gave chase and followed Mr. Interrogator into the bathroom.

I heard four shots ring out, all .223 from James's CAR-15. The interrogator lay dead on the shower floor, never even getting one shot off from his stationary combat "ready" position.

Kurt Muse was eventually located in his cell. He had to cover himself under his mattress so the door could be explosively breached and he could be recovered. He was placed in body armor and a helmet, given specific instructions to do exactly what he was told to without deviation. The call went over the radio that the cargo had been recovered. Now we just needed the EXFIL birds to come get us.

At this point, I was lying out on a balcony, engaging bad guys in the courtyard and in the *Comandancia*, which was about one hundred meters away. I figured if I had to wait for the birds, I might as well continue to neutralize the threat.

I heard the buzzing of the rotor blades as the birds landed on the roof and waited for someone to tap me on the shoulder to tell me it was time to go.

I waited and waited and waited and nothing. Amidst all of the noise, chaos, and darkness, it became evident to me that I was alone! I reached back with my non-firing hand, hoping to feel a team member behind me, but…nothing. I reached back with a leg and tried to sweep and feel for someone…again, nothing.

I heard the PDF sneaking up the stairs, and I thought, "Well, shit."

As I look back to that moment, it reminds me of the scene in *Aliens* when the Marines are barricaded in a room and the aliens are coming in through the ceilings, just feet and seconds away. That's how I felt as I heard the PDF stepping on crushed glass and speaking in Spanish, saying, "*despacio*" ("slowly"), "*con cuidado*" ("be careful"), and "*hay un hombre muy peligroso arriba*" ("There's a badass up there").

Okay, the last line was a joke, but I realized that this might be the part in my life's story where I became a POW and would get to practice all my cool counter-interrogation techniques. Or that this might be the part where I threw down some lead-hate and ran like a scalded dog up the stairs, hoping like hell a ride was waiting for me. I liked option two better.

When I exited the annex, I saw my helo sitting on the roof. I ran over and, to my surprise, someone else was sitting in my seat. I looked around for more seating when the interloper realized he was on the wrong bird. He ran back to his, and I gladly took what was mine, ready to call it a night.

I had no idea it wasn't over yet.

20

When my bird left the roof, the operator on my side and I filled the cars with bullets and exchanged bullets with the ground-floor enemy. As we lifted up and headed back to Howard Air Force Base, we witnessed the fight raging in the streets. At this point, the 193rd had rolled in with their armored personnel carriers mounted with .50 caliber machine guns. The Americans manning these vehicles were not all infantry. Many were cooks, mechanics, and support personnel who had volunteered to drive in and provide blocking positions.

These guys were so excited that they shot the hell out of everything that flashed, including my bird as it lifted off. I remember seeing what looked like flaming basketballs coming at us and zipping under our feet. They were .50 caliber tracers.

We cleared the target area and arrived at the JMAU, a joint medical unit established to receive casualties on the airfield tarmac. We were supposed to be the last bird to arrive, yet we were the only bird to have landed. My team leader told us to sit fast while he conferred with the heads, who had all assembled on the airfield.

When he returned, he yelled at us to reload our weapons because we were going back. Apparently, the helo with Kurt onboard had been shot down and we had to go get him. I wasn't scared until then. We had just flown out of the hornet's nest and now we had to go and stick our peckers into the hive...oh, hell!

It turned out Kurt had been on the first bird off the roof. He had been stuffed in the middle with two operators sitting outside on each pod. Because of the weight, the helo got an awkward running start by skimming the roof and then diving off to pick up air speed and lift. When that happened, the bird received a lot of ground fire from the bottom floor and from the vehicles parked in front of the building. With some amazing flying, the pilots flew down several streets before they crashed.

As we started spinning up, the word came across the radio that Kurt had been recovered and the task force was on its way back. When his bird had crashed, all of the operators aboard were shot or seriously injured. The bird was sitting sideways with the engine running and its blades spinning. Realizing that he was the only conscious survivor, Kurt stepped out of the helicopter, thinking he was the only one alive.

As he moved forward, Tim, my ATL, came to and saw Kurt starting to walk into the rotor blades. Tim jumped up, grabbed Kurt, and pulled him down. This act of courage saved Kurt, but caused Tim to take a rotor strike to the head, shaving off the top of his helmet, knocking him unconscious, and rendering him with a head injury that took him six months to recover from.

People ask me all the time what this experience was like for me. Was I scared? The answer is, no, I wasn't scared, at least not initially. There is a lot of truth to the adage, "Train the way you fight and you will fight the way you train." The night of the rescue seemed like a training mission—except that we were shooting live targets who were shooting back.

Roof of Modelo Prison

Barber Shop in Modelo Prison

High Rise Bldg in Modelo Prison

Bathroom where Interrogator was killed

Guard Tower in Modelo Prison

Annex on roof that I explosively beached to enter Modelo

Prison yard inside Modelo Prison

Breach point on the Annex, where we entered.
The doorway consisted of a steel door with a jail
door six inches in front.

Commanancia across from Modelo Prison

Republica de Panama

Over the Darien Jungle –
one of the most remote and dense jungles in the world.

21

Twenty-one years later, in 2010, I went to Panama on a business trip. I later became the vice president for the same company's critical infrastructure protection division—a position I still hold. While I was in Panama, brokering business deals with local businessmen, I was introduced to Gustavo Perez. Gustavo was the chief of national police for Panama. Because of the nature of the business, he became part of the business discussions, and it soon occurred to me that, in 1989, he had been Manuel Noriega's chief bodyguard and interrogator. In fact, he had been on the run from US forces while trying to protect and hide Noriega. Essentially, he was doing his job at the time like any good soldier would.

I remember when Noriega took refuge in the papal nuncio's residence in downtown Panama. High-rise buildings encircled the compound and we had the place surrounded with snipers, shooters, MPs, infantry, and, of course, the news media.

I was standing on the second floor of a parking garage, looking into the compound. I could clearly see Noriega inside the building with his bodyguards. Often the bodyguards would step out to smoke cigarettes, weapons slung behind them. They would look up and nod to me. I looked down at them and wondered what I would do if I were in their shoes. I guess I probably would have done the same thing—except I didn't smoke. I remember Gustavo coming out and not looking as friendly as his men. I guess he needed to keep his edge in case they had to form up and fight in a hurry. Being cordial in front of his men may have seemed like a weakness.

As I got to know Gustavo, I kind of developed a liking for the guy. He seemed very professional and enjoyed talking to me about the invasion over lunch or dinner. It was interesting listening to his perspective and the things he did to resist us. From what I know about him, he was a soldier who fought for his country. He was there to win, just as we were.

He once told me about an incident where he rigged a house with high explosives. The house had bags containing millions of dollars inside—Noriega's get-away money. They learned of an impending raid on the way, and quickly abandoned the house. Wanting to kill as many Americans as possible once they entered, Gustavo waited as long as he could to arm the system before leaving. I remember the mission well, and the house never detonated. Fearing he would not make it off the target alive if he waited any longer, Gustavo had abandoned the house and linked up with the rest of his bodyguard detail. The US military secured the house and money, but the search for Noriega continued.

Paratroopers and the Jungle Girl

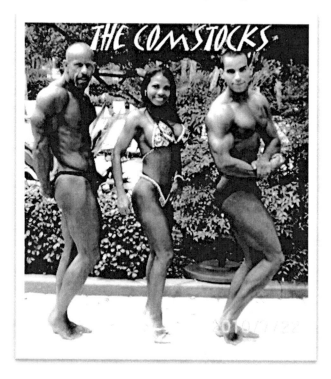

Me, my wife, and my son after a body building competition
in Orlando, Florida.

22

My wife, Miroslava, is from Panama. She is of Panamanian and Chinese descent. Her family lived in the jungle on a small farm near the Chagres River. Every time I watch the movie *Apocalypto*, my wife reminds me that her family's ancestry is tied to the Mayans. So when I think about my wife's life growing up in the jungles, I see her as this hot naked chick. That keeps my marriage to her a little more interesting, if you're old enough to know what I mean! I call my wife my "Jungle Girl" because that's pretty much what she was growing up.

While the invasion was underway, she had no idea, nor did her family, what was going on in the country. They were a poor family consisting of twelve children. They lived off the land, hunting, fishing, and gathering food from the forest in order to survive.

She and her sisters gathered berries and fruit. They got water from the river in which they also washed their clothes. One day, a platoon of American soldiers from the 82nd Airborne Division patrolled by, ordering her out of the water. She was a young woman at the time, bathing nude in the river. After sensing, and seeing, that she was embarrassed, they allowed her to get dressed and had her lead them to her home where they detained her father and older brothers to determine whether or not they were combatants. Eventually, the Americans realized they were simple men trying to take care of their family and they released them. My wife doesn't harbor any bad feelings and knows they were just doing their jobs, maybe a bit more than that when they stared at her nude, but nonetheless no one was hurt.

My German mother once told me a similar story about growing up in WWII. The American soldiers would sweep through her village and enter her house. After detaining my grandfather (Opa), they would make themselves at home. They took over the house, lying on the beds and furniture, posting sentries on lookout on the roof and in over-watch positions. My grandfather had a wine cellar where he kept his favorite wines. The Americans would take the wine, set the bottles on the table in front of him and make my grandfather drink from every bottle to ensure that it didn't contain poison. After drinking multiple gulps of wine, he would get intoxicated and lose all sense of his family's disposition. Although none took advantage of him or his family, the situation was quite inconvenient. Once the Americans were satisfied that it was safe, they would drink the wine until they were drunk and help themselves to all the food.

Once they were satiated and had no need to remain in the house, they would leave and move on to the next mission.

Eagles 'R' Chickens

Eagle-buzzard-chicken, 1990

23

Five months after the Modelo Prison raid, I ended up back in Central America to conduct jungle training. My unit and I went to a remote jungle to practice survival techniques, including hunting and living off the land. Once broken up into teams, we were separated and instructed to stay in the jungle for three days without rations. We had to build our own shelters and gather our own food.

While I was out with a teammate, looking for something to eat, we walked all day before I finally saw something worth shooting and eating. It was some kind of black eagle, or maybe a buzzard. Either way, I was thinking…chicken! I sent a .223 round through his body and put him in my pants' cargo pocket for transport.

A couple of hours later, right before we reached our camp, I started to cross a small river that had large river rocks. As I was crossing, I looked down and saw the most amazing sight ever—a river otter the size of a German shepherd swimming underwater like a dolphin. Because he was massive and swam underwater so effortlessly, I didn't realize he was an otter at first. Then he surfaced about forty meters away, his head popping out of the water with these big, chestnut-like eyes looking at me. I didn't even think about it; I just knew I was hungry and he looked tasty, so I opened up with my CAR-15 and tried to send him to the light.

He jumped out of the water and ran up the river on the rocks like a cat. I was letting bullets go as fast as I could press the trigger and yet, *nada*! I missed, he lived, and PETA can relax if they are reading this.

After I was finished with my hunt, I started to have second thoughts about what I had done. I felt really bad about shooting the bird-eagle-buzzard-chicken, and the otter, who was probably just going home from a day of fishing.

At this time in my life superstition really gave me something to think about, and I thought karma was going to get me for sure. Man, was I right!

The next morning, my group moved out to a clearing that was to be our helicopter-landing zone (HLZ). It was a small clearing, capable of supporting two UH-60 Blackhawk helicopters at one time. We had three birds coming in to pick us up, and at this point, we had received an intelligence report saying an enclave of bad guys might be hanging out about ten minutes away in an old gold mine. The plan was to land in the area, investigate, and see how things unfolded.

As we staged in pick-up zone (PZ) posture, we were locked and loaded and ready for a fight.

Eagles Down

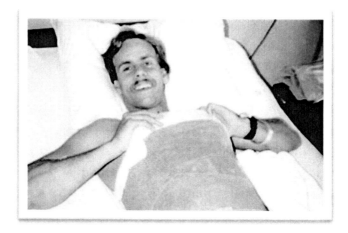

Pink body cast after the Helo crash.
It was the orthopedic surgeon's idea to humble us!

24

The first two helos landed and my team entered the first one. We had a total of fifteen personnel and equipment (PAX), including the four crewmembers who had flown down. The auxiliary fuel tank in the back of the cargo area was approximately two-and-a-half by four feet high and eight feet wide.

We packed in tight, feet out the doors, sitting on the floors, on ammo cans, and anywhere else we could squeeze our asses. I took a knee and grasped two cargo rings that were attached to the ceiling to stabilize myself.

We lifted off and were underway, when at 206 feet above ground level (AGL) the number one engine had a catastrophic failure. It made a weird vacuum sound, and immediately I could feel the bird losing lift. It felt like I was on an elevator going down. Simultaneously, the audible alarms activated in the cockpit and the crew chief excitedly motioned for us all to sit and hang on.

Before that day, and every time I flew, any time the helicopter acted strangely in flight, I would always look at the crew chief to see his reaction. If he was calm, I was calm.

I also mentally rehearsed what I would do if the helo were to crash, but the reality is, in a situation like that, there isn't much you can do but pray. But my thought was that maybe I could do enough to minimize my impact and enhance my survivability. So I developed a sequence of action in my head through autogenic conditioning.

The first step was to remove my headgear. The second was to un-sling my weapon and detach it from my body. The third step was to remove my load-bearing equipment, and the fourth was to grasp the cargo rings above.

My thought was that, in the event I survived the crash, I didn't want to get hung up by the equipment strapped to my body.

Grasping the cargo rings would give my body more anchor points to resist the inertia with as the helo came to a dynamic stop. I figured that even if this was futile, it would give me something to do and take my mind off the pain to come.

I did exactly as I had always planned. I had mentally rehearsed this contingency so many times that I did it without thinking about it. My mind was engaged in the here and now. It was surreal and scary as hell. Trees, easily several hundred feet tall, snapped the bird's rotor blades at the hubs. We were in free fall through the jungle when the helo rolled to the left. The guys in the door on that side hung on to the cargo strap so they wouldn't fall out. I remember hanging vertically by the cargo rings with my legs hanging down through the door, looking at the jungle floor rushing at us. Tree limbs were crashing through the windshield, metal was creaking under torsion, and shit was flying everywhere.

25

Almost immediately, the bird righted itself and we crashed belly down. The impact was severe. I was knocked unconscious but awoke soon after impact. I was flat on my back, looking at the ceiling in the center of the bird. I heard a hissing sound and the crackling of fire burning in the transmission. I looked left and right and down by my feet, and to my shock and horror, it seemed I was the only guy left in the bird. While looking around, I felt this terrible pain in my lower back that I can only describe as feeling like a monster was twisting my body in half and ripping it apart. I later learned that the pain I suffered stemmed from a broken back. I had crushed L-2 and L-3 and came close to severing my spinal cord.

I rolled over slowly, got to my hands and knees, and crawled to the edge of the right door. What I hadn't noticed at first was an operator lying in a pile behind me toward the cockpit. He was unconscious with a shattered pelvis and bleeding to death. Both crew chiefs sitting behind the mini guns had been ejected out of their windows and over the guns—I still don't know how that happened. Both pilots were still in their seats and unconscious.

I made it to the edge of the door and fell out onto the ground where I crawled about four more feet before rolling to my back. I looked to my right and saw one of the crew chiefs unconscious, his face covered in blood. His bottom lip was ripped off his face and lying on his left cheekbone. To my left I heard the beacon alarm on one of the AN/PRC-112 survival radios that we all carried. The medic on my team—Tom, a good friend and mentor of mine—activated the alarm to notify any potential commercial aircraft in the area that we had an emergency.

At this point, he and I were the only two conscious. I was in so much pain that I couldn't think straight. When I saw Tom, all I could think was that he was a medic and that he could help me. I selfishly asked for his help, and he responded: "Bubba, there is nothing that I can do for you. My leg is broken and I can't move." Once again, I thought to myself, "Well, shit."

Soon everyone was beginning to wake up, and all I heard were the groans of injured men. I figured I had better lie still to avoid further injury.

The other helicopters and the rest of the troop returned to the original HLZ and then cut their way into the jungle to recover us. When they arrived, the medics began triage and organized the rest of the troop to move all of the wounded back to the HLZ for dust-off at a military hospital about an hour-and-half flight away.

As I lay on the ground, the rest of the men worked steadily to get the injured loaded on spine boards. Eventually, everyone was on the way to the HLZ...except for me.

I lay there, stoned out of my gourd with morphine, watching the last guy in what we call a file formation head off into the jungle. At first I thought someone was coming back to get me. Then I realized they forgot I was still lying there, and had no intention of coming back.

They were about forty-five meters away when I yelled, "Hey!"

The last guy in formation turned and I heard him yell to the others, "Oh shit, we left Comstock!" Four of them came back with a spine board. They were very apologetic and I was too gooned out on painkillers to give them any flak.

Within a few of hours, I found myself on a gurney in the hospital. It was Mother's Day 1990, a Sunday, so the skeleton staff on duty found themselves overwhelmed when they realized they had fifteen badly injured men to triage and save.

I was lying on the gurney in the hallway, and the morphine was starting to wear off. My good friend Pepper was nearby waiting to assist the nurses.

His name isn't really Pepper, but because of the following incident, I have to protect his identity.

While lying naked under a sheet on the gurney, unable to move because of a broken back, I felt this weird sensation in my groin area, more specifically, on my junk. It felt like an itching and tingling that was all too familiar.

If you spend enough time in the field, eventually you'll experience the bites of ticks, chiggers, leeches, spiders, and other evil creatures. I knew from experience that something was going on down south that involved creatures sucking and biting with bad intentions.

I asked Pepper to come over. I said, "Pepper, something's biting me on my balls and I would like for you to take a gander and confirm or deny my inclination."

Pepper was one of the most jovial men that I have ever known. He always laughed and was never visibly upset about anything. When I made this request, he giggled with embarrassment, saying, "I can't do that. That's too awkward."

I looked at him with panic in my eyes. "Pepper, please, just take a look and tell me what's going on."

He giggled some more before finally agreeing. He looked up and down the hall to make sure no one was watching and then lifted the sheet.

His eyes got real big as he cried out, "Oh, shit!" My first thought was that he was pretty impressed with the display of equipment, though I would rather he had not commented. He looked at me, eyes wide, "Dude, you're covered in ticks!"

Now why in the hell did all these ticks climb onto my body while I was lying in the jungle and decide to bypass normal dining spots like the armpits, scalp, and legs, and move as a unit to one central location and attack my tool?

"Pepper, you gotta get 'em off me, now. Who knows what those little vampires are going to do to me!" The panic was obvious in my voice, I'm sure—it's not every day you break your back and have a colony of ticks take up residence on your junk.

After a bit of discourse, Pepper reluctantly agreed to remove the pesky little bloodsuckers from my reproductive essence—but with two conditions. First, we would never discuss what happened with each other, and second, I had to promise never to tell anyone about it. I gladly agreed and told him to get busy!

Pepper raised the sheet, put his head under it, and got to work removing the ticks. He got 'em all and I thanked him from the bottom of my pubis. Since that day, I have only told the story maybe five times and never used his real name. If he's reading this, I hope he's well and knows that his secret is still safe with me.

While five of us suffered broken backs and the rest walked away with various injuries, ranging from shattered pelvises and broken legs and arms and ribs, to disfigurations and a multitude of other superficial and internal injuries, that helo crash paralyzed two men for life. For one unfortunate operator, this was his third helo crash in six months. The second was at Modelo Prison when he was shot down, and the first was during a rehearsal for Modelo. The third crash paralyzed this American hero for life, and yet America will never know his name for his and his family's safety. He was one of America's silent warriors and served out of patriotism and not glory.

"With every triumph I am empowered, with every failure I am resolute—I will never quit!"

Yosemite Sam's Advice

Blackhawk crash, Panama, Mother's Day, 1990

26

In my twenty-nine years working as either a soldier or a paramilitary contractor, I have had the opportunity to experience combat. I also had the chance to confirm what I already knew about myself as a man. Some men never reveal their true characters nor do they know their true characters until they are placed in a situation where their life is at stake. We as humans tend to speculate and wonder what we would do if we found ourselves in a situation that would inevitably end in violence. When I was eighteen years old in the 82nd ABN 325th Infantry I always wondered what I would do once I was in combat. Would I freeze up or would I fight without hesitation? I knew in my mind what I wanted to do, but I also knew that circumstances tend to influence one's courage.

Yosemite Sam—the main instructor in my Delta operator training course—always told us, "Run the situation. Don't let the situation run you." I still live by that mantra and say it to myself when things get confusing or dangerous.

When men are put in the position where they have to choose to fight despite the possibility of being killed, in my experience, three kinds of characters arise.

The first is the warrior who courageously meets the threat head-on and is willing to fight to the death if needed. Courage is the strength one musters from within to do something even when they are fraught with fear. Fearlessness is a juvenile trait. Those who are fearless are not wise enough to understand that they could be in jeopardy. I will take the courageous to combat over the fearless any day.

The second kind is the man who doesn't know what to do and doesn't have the mettle to fight and kill. He postures and shoots his weapon ineffectively over the heads of the enemy, or he retreats to the rear, lying low until the fight is over. With training and experience, this man, sometimes, can be taught to fight with commitment.

The third man is the coward. He is the one who makes up excuses for why he shouldn't participate in an operation. The third man is what I call a poser. You see them from time to time. They have all the "cool guy" gear, tend to talk to impress, and then when it is time to saddle up and leave the wire, they come up with a hundred reasons they would be "adding value" by staying behind in support of your ass while you're out in Indian country. It's just as well to me: if you're a coward, and don't have the fortitude to fight alongside me, I don't need you anyway—you're a liability.

Being afraid to die is not the same as being prepared to die. Everyone alive has some fear of dying. That is what keeps us vigilant throughout life, but those who are prepared to die have made peace with themselves. These are people who are satisfied with the life they have lived, know those they leave behind will be taken care of, and will go out gloriously knowing they died for righteous reasons. Death is a part of living that we must all embrace someday.

Sadr City

Jockn'n up for a midnight raid on Sadr City, Iraq 2007

27

I had a tendency to rotate between Afghanistan and Iraq almost every two months. I was deployed overseas seven to eight months out of the year. When you have two children in college and two still at home, you have to work to keep the income stream flowing. Aside from needing the money, I loved the work. I was bred to be a soldier—it didn't seem right for me to stand idly on the sidelines, watching two wars fought without me.

My mother would always ask, "Why do you have to do it? Why do you have to go and fight, leaving your family behind?"

My answer was always the same. "If I don't do it, who will?" Not many people out there have the will or the skills to do this job. I do this because I love the American way of life. I love my family and friends, and I do this for those who share the same values as me. But I also do this for those who spit on me in the airport and burn the flag. I do it because I am a man and an American warrior.

On my next rotation to Baghdad, Iraq, I was part of an ACES (Asymmetrical Clandestine Elite Services) counter-insurgency team. Our mission was to hunt high-value targets (HVTs), using various intelligence collection platforms and human intelligence (HUMINT). We would conduct nightly raids to kill or capture HVTs and those deemed as leaders or significant operational assets—the brains of the beast.

One night in Baghdad, we left our compound around 2300 hours, heading to Sadr City to conduct two missions back-to-back. The house of an insurgent commander who was running IED operations against US convoys was the first target. The second was a mosque where insurgents were running operations and had a possible weapons cache on site.

We left our compound in armored vehicles and soon approached a road intersection where a group of approximately fifty Iraqis was threatening three Iraqi police officers.

As we drove through the crowd, an Iraqi opened fire on the officers. Without delay, our top gunners assailed the group with .50 caliber M-2 machine guns. Though we didn't know what the altercation was about, if an Iraqi opened fire around us, killing police officers no less, then we were going to make that Iraqi and his supporters go away.

We continued driving through the crowd without stopping. Stopping a vehicle was bad practice, especially at night. We had to get to a target area as quickly as possible, because there were always active and passive observers watching our movements, and as soon as a convoy or patrol left their wire, the insurgents would broadcast a call notifying everyone of the size of the element and the direction of travel. This gave the opposition time to evacuate their safe houses, emplace IEDs and ambushes, and better prepare to attack patrols coming and going.

Another reason to never stop or drive too slowly was the risk of losing a vehicle and its occupants to a rogue RPG or a hasty enemy ambush. That causes a *Black Hawk Down* scenario—with all efforts going toward extracting dead and wounded soldiers and equipment back to base while under duress.

Sadr City was a very dangerous area in Baghdad. It was an enclave for bad guys, fraught with IEDs and choke points intended to take out US forces. For the most part, US forces stayed away at night. If they did enter, they would stay on the fringes with heavy air support.

As the war went on, the insurgents became more creative in their use of terrain, moveable obstacles, choke points, communication, and coordination when ambushing US military. On one occasion, a mounted patrol entered a roadway lined on both sides with adjoining buildings and structures. The insurgents barricaded both ends of the roads, effectively boxing in the vehicles. They then began their attack from the buildings and ends of the street.

Armored vehicles are more vulnerable on their tops (thinner armor and limited vertical view by the occupants), making them easy to engage with RPGs and machine-gun fire as the troops exit the vehicles to fight or move obstacles.

As we rolled into Sadr City, dismounting several blocks away from the target house, we placed snipers on the roofs to provide cover fire for our movement on foot. When we reached our destination, we lined up and stacked the doors for explosive entry. On a countdown, the charges went off, causing the doors to blow off. The Iraqi mercenary teams went through the house like ants overrunning a termite mound. I came in behind my men to oversee their activities, providing direction as needed.

I always found it interesting that we would spend countless hours training the Iraqi mercs to conduct close-quarter battle, which always looked very regimented and fluid during training, yet in combat, their technique did not look anything like what we had taught them.

This wasn't necessarily a bad thing. My theory is they were so amped up on entry, wanting to kill and not be killed, that the procedures were left at the door. Instinct to simply charge through the structure with speed and while maintaining the element of surprise took over. They would enter the bottom floor and within seconds be on the third floor or roof. It was amazing how fast these guys moved.

Once I was inside, I heard shots from the roof and knew something terrible had happened. When I reached the roof, I found the dead body of the adversary we had come for. With three satellite phones in his pocket, he had tried to evade us by running across the flat rooftops. What he did not count on were the snipers lying in wait to curtail his plans.

He had taken a single round from a Winchester .300 Magnum through his left shoulder. It traveled through his lungs and heart, killing him instantly. It was an interesting kill because there were no visible signs of blood, though he was wearing a white dishdash. The bullet had gone through the deltoid straight into the thoracic cavity. The shot shut his heart down so fast there was no time to pump blood out of the wounds, and any bleeding he did have was internal. I had to check to make sure he was dead, in case it was a ruse and he was planning to kill me.

I flicked him in the eye and there was no response. He looked so peaceful, almost as if he were asleep.

We snapped pictures of anything found on the target, including the dead man. We took his sat-phones, which would later be exploited for telephone numbers leading us to his counterparts. We left his body behind because we had no room in our vehicles. Moreover, we figured it would be a nice reminder to his cronies that they were not untouchable.

In Iraq and Afghanistan, we had a limited window of time in which to operate. The sun started rising around 0400 hours, and we were like vampires if caught outside. Daylight and the increase of human activity put us in grave danger, simply because the enemy could see us.

28

It was 0130 hours when we loaded into our vehicles, leaving time to go to the mosque and service it before we needed to be back in base. At the mosque, we sent in our Iraqi allies first. After a thorough search, we found nothing. It was no surprise— sometimes you find a "dry hole." Depending on the source of intelligence, which in this case was HUMINT, much of the information received can be false or dated.

We had one very reliable source when I was in Tikrit, Saddam Hussein's hometown, although he had the bad habit of claiming certain individuals were bad guys, when in fact, they were just having a dispute and he wanted us to arrest or kill them. We caught on to his game early, though, and he did help us land some legitimate targets.

One day he came in and said his nephew saw Saddam in a pick-up truck at a gas station. This seemed odd to me since there was a twenty-five-million-dollar bounty on Saddam's head.

Why didn't his nephew jump on that opportunity?

The reality was, like most people in Iraq, he didn't know about the bounty.

My replacement pulled Saddam Hussein out of his underground hideout a few days later.

After we loaded our vehicles to head back to camp from Sadr City, we received radio intercepts that two separate groups were setting up IEDs on our anticipated routes back. Both groups blew themselves up trying to arm their own systems. Talk about karma.

As we started heading back, our ISR bird (intelligence, surveillance, and reconnaissance) above reported that a black Mercedes was speeding down a dirt road toward us. We communicated between twenty-one armored vehicles and everyone was on alert. All the vehicles had an ISR video feed, so everyone could see what the ISR bird was seeing.

The Mercedes abruptly stopped in a cloud of dust at a four-way intersection. A few seconds later, it sped away in another direction and we continued our route of travel. As, one by one, each vehicle negotiated the intersection, a massive IED detonated in front of my vehicle. It created a crater that was six feet deep and at least thirty feet in diameter. When the IED detonated, all hell broke loose on the right flank.

The road we were traveling on ran in front of a line of apartments for at least a mile. We received fire from AK-47s and RPGs from every balcony, corner, and rooftop in the area. It was an amazing sight, considering I was buttoned up inside an armored vehicle, unable to shoot back. All I could do was look out the window in bewilderment, watching the muzzle flashes from the buildings. This was no doubt a coordinated attack on the enemy's behalf. They had predicted our route of travel, armed an IED, and notified every combatant in the mile-long apartment complex to shut off their lights and ambush us as we drove by. Our top-mounted gunners on the .50 caliber M-2s and Mark-19 automatic grenade launchers racked up all the kills that night. I remember an insurgent running out with an RPG about fifty meters away and our gunner sending him to Allah with a .50 cal Ma-Deuce.

After the excitement, we made it back to base before sunrise to start sensitive site exploitation (SSE), the process of collecting, recording, and cataloging evidence, weapons, photos, and documents recovered on a target. Once we finished, we turned over any personnel under control (PUCs) to the detention center. Then we all headed off to bed to rest up for our first operations order later in the afternoon.

Any time we conducted an operation, we received heavy mortar fire at base camp in retaliation. After a while we just learned to sleep through the attacks. If we wanted to get some rest, we had to take it and dismiss the enemy.

Tikrit

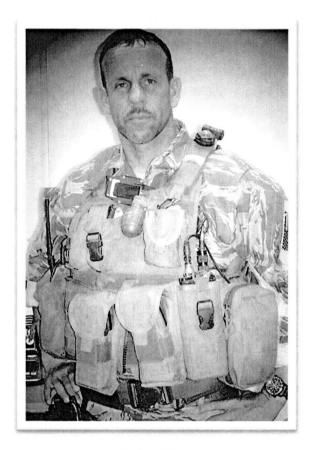

Baghdad, Iraq

29

There was never a dull day in Tikrit, Iraq. Everyone there was pro-Saddam and anti-American. There were gun battles with our perimeter security around the clock. I remember on two occasions insurgents shooting down helicopters that were landing in our base. It was the Wild Wild West.

About three kilometers away, an 82 mm mortar would rain steel on us every night. The mortar was underground, covered by a tarp during the day. At night, the insurgents would go to the mortar pit and launch their nightly allocation of rounds at us. Then one night, an AH-64 Apache pilot and gunner dialed in on their position and serviced them with a hellfire missile and a smile.

One day, the senior paramilitary officer I was working with decided we needed to go to Balad, Iraq, about sixty-five miles south of Tikrit, to pick up an alternator from a destroyed Toyota Land Cruiser. We had two armored vehicles on base—a Mercedes G5 and an up-armored Toyota Land Cruiser, and the Land Cruiser was out of commission because of a bad alternator.

Five of us were going on this alternator hunt: one ACES operative (me), two security specialists, one US interpreter (interpreters are sometimes called "terps"), and the chief paramilitary officer. We briefed the unit troop commander on our planned route of travel and destination, including our anticipated return time, so that in case we disappeared, they could file missing persons reports. Before we departed, the chief suggested that the interpreter, who normally rode behind the driver's seat, ride in the armored G5 while he and I drove the faulty Land Cruiser.

We left around 8:00 AM, expecting to travel one way for about four hours to Balad. The ride down was very scenic. We drove parallel to the Tigris River, which was lined with date palm groves and agricultural fields being irrigated from the river. The drive down was uneventful until about thirty minutes after we passed through Samara.

We drove through a small town and I saw Iraqi men filing out of the stores and surrounding buildings. Right about then, the first bullet glanced off the window next to my head. The sound of the bullet just nicking the window was deafening, leaving my left ear ringing for a couple of hours. We never slowed down, and we drove out of the town as fast as we could without crashing.

We reached Balad and recovered the golden alternator for which we had risked our lives. I must admit, I thought this was a stupid thing to do, but I had been ready to get out from behind the HESCO sand barriers and take a drive.

After a two-hour visit, we got back on the road heading home. Driving along the Tigris River on a two-lane hardball road, which twisted through an open area with rice fields on both sides, we passed a US military mounted patrol consisting of one M-113 armored personnel carrier (APC) and two Humvees—one on point and one in trail.

A few minutes later, we ran up on a slower moving vehicle on the road in front of us, and the G5 passed at the first opportunity. I waited until the road straightened before I made my move. The Toyota Land Cruiser I was driving had a 305-cubic-inch V-8 with a five-speed manual overdrive transmission. Because it was unarmored, it could easily keep up with the armored G5.

I downshifted to third gear and passed the car, which only had one person inside. As soon as the right rear corner of my car was in line with the other car's front left corner—at about forty-five miles per hour—all hell broke loose.

The windows of the Land Cruiser were blown out, and the tires flattened. The pressure changed suddenly when the windows blew out, reminding me of what it's like to sit in the back of a C-141 as the ramp lowers before a parachute jump.

Disconcerted, I first thought we were taking fire from the vehicle we had just passed. However, it occurred to me that the ambush was on my side of the vehicle. Chief was reaching for his radio to notify the lead vehicle that we were in contact. By the time he started to transmit, I had floored the gas pedal and passed the G5. As we went roaring by, the other half of the team saw the damage to my vehicle and knew we had to get the hell out of dodge. We cleared the ambush and drove for about another half-mile before I had to pull my bullet-riddled vehicle over.

30

Now, of all the firefights, ambushes, and near death experiences I have had, this is the only one that truly freaked me out. It rattled my cage, but not because I was scared. Hell, I've been in a lot scarier situations (like when I was seven years old and had to dance in the Nutcracker ballet in front of hundreds of parents without a dance partner). No, what had me amped up and out of sorts was that I was hit and did not see it coming, nor was I mentally prepared for it. I was figuratively asleep at the wheel, enjoying a Sunday drive through an Iraqi warzone, probably picking my noise.

We pulled over in an area where many people roamed on foot and in their vehicles. We were still in a rural area with thick vegetation and the same groves of date palms. Upon dismounting, we assessed the damage. Chief decided we could change the tires on my vehicle and continue driving. Meanwhile, I was concerned that we were sitting ducks. If we didn't move soon, the five of us wouldn't be capable of fighting off our attackers, who would probably approach from within the palm groves.

To make matters worse, that particular vehicle required a coupler attached to a crowbar to break the lug nuts. The coupler wasn't in the tool kit. When I had inventoried the vehicle, I added any items needed in case of an emergency—tow-straps, oil, gas, tools, duct tape, fix-a-flat cans, that sort of thing. I was completely unaware this vehicle would need that coupler.

How were we supposed to change the tires without the coupler? I adamantly suggested we blow up the vehicle in place and pile into the G5. I had been ambushed twice that day, and I was ready to go to base and call it a wrap. Chief was determined to save the vehicle because we didn't have enough vehicles to begin with. I thought we might actually die saving a car! That would have made for an interesting eulogy: "Dale Comstock died as he valorously tried to recover a wounded Toyota Land Cruiser, in order to save the US government $22,545."

It didn't make sense for all five of us to be working around the vehicles, so I moved behind a mound about twenty meters away to pull security. The sun was setting and soon the boogieman would be upon us. I didn't like the atmosphere.

At about the same time, I saw the US military patrol coming down the road. I flagged them down and asked the first lieutenant in charge if he could have his unit set in over-watch positions and pull security while we worked on the vehicles. He was happy to help, and we worked on the lug nuts with sockets and a ratchet.

About an hour later, we finally got back on the road. When we arrived on the base, I went into the tactical operations center (TOC) and told the unit troop commander, the same one I had informed when we left, what happened to us. His response: "Oh, that area's known as Ambush Alley. We never take that road!"

I stared at him incredulously; I couldn't help but wonder why he didn't mention this tid-bit of useful information before we left on our adventure.

When inspecting the damage and size of the bullet holes to the Toyota, I plucked a 7.62 x 54 mm PKM—a Russian machine gun—bullet out of one of my tires. Looking at the rear window, I noticed a bullet had just missed my head. It went through the glass behind me and out the back of the vehicle.

I called my interpreter over and asked him to sit in his usual seat. He was shocked to see that, based on the bullet's line of flight, it would have gone through his head! Good call, Chief!

Malik Maherin

Standing before a valley strewn with Russian mines, on the way to Kunduz, Afghanistan to hit a target.

31

Malik is an Arabic title, meaning chieftain or king, bestowed on the senior man in a tribe or village. Malik Maherin was an Afghan National Police (ANP) chief. He worked under the Afghan government, controlling most of the Afghan National Police around the northeast border of Afghanistan and Pakistan, and was presumably a United States ally.

In reality, we knew he worked for the Taliban. He was responsible for subverting US efforts in the region and intimidating the local populace to keep them from working with Americans or Karzai's government. His police were henchman who carried out his dirty deeds.

Malik's compound was located across the Kunar River near the Pakistan border. He had ANP checkpoints on the bridge that crossed over the river. Any time Americans crossed, the ANP would call ahead and warn him of our approach. He would then evacuate his compound until he knew it was safe to return.

Due to the bridge, and the ever-loyal ANP, he was a hard guy to catch. I gave the situation a lot of thought, and finally came up with a plan to capture him. It would require a bit of preparation, but it would work.

His compound was located northeast of the bridge in a deep valley near Pakistan. A north-south running road paralleled the east side of the riverbank.

I decided to take a force of sixty Afghan mercs across the bridge and drive south about three kilometers to a small village. At around 1400 hours, we set up a vehicle checkpoint (VCP) on the road. I pushed all of our vehicles into a defensive perimeter about one hundred meters in diameter. We spent the day searching vehicles, hoping the ANP goons manning the bridge would tell

Malik and he would be comfortable staying home, figuring the vehicles were all we were interested in.

We continued searching vehicles into the night. As it got late, I pulled the perimeter in tighter and organized a dismounted patrol. The patrol headed out north then east, walking six kilometers over hills and mountains to assault Malik's compound.

As far as the ANP and locals were concerned, we were still there in force, conducting VCP procedures. In the meantime, I was leading forty-eight Afghans over hill and dale to some high ground overlooking the valley and Malik's compound.

The plan was to wait for an Army Special Forces team of Green Berets to roll on to the bridge and detain all of the ANP before they could make a phone call once they had noticed our real intentions.

Simultaneously, at around 0200 hours, we descended the hill beside the compound and encircled it.

Placing and setting a door charge on the main entrance, I fired on a countdown. The charge went off and we entered the compound, thoroughly surprising Malik. We got our man and conducted SSE.

By first light, we pulled off the target and were headed back to camp. About two hundred meters away from the compound we stopped and could hear women wailing. One of the operatives in the truck said this was a good sign—Afghan women wail when they know a husband is a bad guy and has been captured. It was just another gloomy day of living alone on the fringes of Afghan society.

The Deer Hunter

Afghanistan, 2008

32

As I mentioned before, operators in the Army Special Operations are just American patriots. They are your average guys except that they have extraordinary determination, pay close attention to details, can act in the absence of orders, and do the right thing even when no one is looking.

With over twenty-nine years in this line of work, I found myself bouncing around the Special Operations community, whether I was in Special Forces, Delta, Asymmetrical Clandestine Elite Services (ACES), or operating as a mercenary under my own banner. I found myself in the action mostly because of military obligations or economic necessity. Most importantly, I always found myself surrounded by some of the most special people in the world—soldiers. I love soldiers for the kind of people they are, regardless of what army they fight for and what ethnicity they are. They are of a warrior class that will give their lives for their country, their people, and their way of life. There is nothing nobler than the warrior who is willing to die for a cause. Than the man who is willing to leave his wife, children, and family behind so that a stranger may keep his and live in peace.

After some time in the Unit, I got the opportunity to be a cadre member for our selection course. I was now on the other side—giving stone-faced looks and concise, exact instructions, while continuously analyzing the candidates for their suitability to be operators.

Selection was a tough time for students. The course challenging and demanded mental and physical toughness. One of the most memorable times I had while acting as cadre happened at a location way in the mountains: Students were being released individually to move by foot, using a map for guidance, to another location. I drove a covered pick-up truck to the drop-off point, with eight students in the back. When I arrived, another operator was at my drop-off point, releasing his candidates. I called ahead, and he told me over the radio that there was an injured deer nearby. I remember thinking, "So what?" and wondering why he didn't just put the deer out of its misery.

This particular operator did not impress me, or anyone else. He soon got fired because his performance fell way short of the 110-percent-a-day benchmark that SGM "A" told me was required to stay employed when I first arrived. In fact, I think the guy's output was about thirty percent a week, if it was warm and sunny.

I showed up as he was starting to leave, and he pointed out the deer lying next to a tree about twenty-five meters away. Needless to say, he didn't hang around to help. Thinking back, I suspect the guy knew of my take-no-prisoners attitude and didn't want to stay and watch me send Bambi to the light.

I released all of my candidates at about ten-minute intervals so they would have to travel alone. After I sent the last candidate on his way, I checked on the condition of the deer. It looked like the night before he had been hit by a truck, severing his two hind legs. It was obvious the ol' boy was going to die a slow miserable death in the woods unless I intervened.

I went back to my truck and all I could find was a crowbar and my Swiss army knife. I decided this was about as deadly as I could get and that it would have to do.

I returned to the deer with the plan of bludgeoning him to death, hopefully with one swift blow from the crowbar. As I approached and was about fifteen feet away, the little booger got up and ran faster on his two front legs than I could on my two.

We went at a sprint through the woods, his crippled ass putting time and space between us. He ran to the edge of the woods and onto a hardtop road. He made a right turn and ran directly down the center of the road on the double yellow lines. I stayed hot on his ass, and as I got about four feet behind him, I started to swing the crowbar at his head. I kept missing! I yelled at him, "Hey, buddy, I'm just trying to help. This will be a lot easier if you just stop!"

Finally, I was making up distance and I got a flush hit on the back of his brain-housing group. That was enough to stun him, forcing him to slow down.

With the crowbar in my left hand and my Swiss army knife in my right, not breaking stride, I jumped on his back, as if I were climbing on a horse, and brought him to his belly. Like a ninja, I dropped the crowbar and grabbed him around his snout with my free hand. Pulling his head back to my chest, I cut his throat from one side of his neck to the other and held his head close so that he could bleed out.

When he finally died, I looked up and saw one of my candidates. He had gotten disoriented and returned, and he was now standing about fifteen meters away, with map and weapon at his side, looking as if he'd just seen an alien eat a human. I shouted, "What're you looking at?" He didn't even respond. He turned and ran into the woods as if I were coming after him next. I can just imagine the story he told his fellow candidates around the fire that night.

33

I had the weekend off and my girlfriend at the time came to see me the next day. We were in the mountains and it was wintertime. She and I had spent the night at a local ski lodge and resort, which one small paved road ran in and out of. Signs everywhere warned of deer crossing on the road. I was driving a brand new Mustang GT with a custom paint job and wheels, so I intentionally drove less than twenty miles per hour.

As we were creeping along, two bucks ran from the left side of the road across to the other side. The first buck ran right in front of the car. The second idiot obviously didn't see a three-thousand-pound, fire-engine red car in front of him, and ran right into the left front quarter panel of my car. He was traveling so fast, when he hit my car, he launched vertically about twelve feet in the air. He was so high up that looking directly out of the windshield we couldn't see him until he landed on my roof. At this point, my girlfriend came unglued and screamed.

When he hit the car, red paint chips splattered the windshield. The buck knocked my outside mirror off, slashed my left front tire, knocked out the head light, ripped off the rocker panel on the bottom of the car, and damaged the hood, the quarter panel, and the top of the car.

He slid down my driver's side door and landed in the street then rose up on his hind legs with his tongue out like a stallion. He did this kind of moonwalk backward and fell down a hill into some underbrush. My girlfriend was coming unraveled next to me, sobbing. I, on the other hand, was pissed and cursing. This hairy jaywalker had just destroyed my phallic symbol, my pride and joy…my steel horse!

I got out of the car and opened the hatch, looking for a knife in my toolbox so I could go down the hill and do what I do—cut deer's throats and put them out of their misery. I figured I'd had plenty of practice the day before, and that this should be easy—assuming he didn't get up on four good legs and fight back.

My girlfriend asked, "What are you looking for?"

"A knife," I replied, throwing things out of my toolbox.

"What for?" She was still sobbing.

I returned with, "To cut his throat!"

She said (get ready for this), "Why? He didn't mean to hit your car!"

I stood up, bumping the back of my head on the hatch, and looked at her in total disbelief. "Really?" I could not believe her! "Now that you said that, I think I ought to just let him live!"

After that brief intellectual discourse, I walked to the edge of the road with a razor knife, ready to do the deed.

I love hearing men brag about how many deer they've killed during hunting season.

When they ask me, I respond by saying, "Shit, I killed two in two days."

They nod their heads, unimpressed, until I add, "Anyone can shoot a damn deer licking a salt rock, or taking a dump, or eating breakfast. But it takes a real hunter like me to run them down on foot and cut their throats with a three-inch Swiss army knife."

I usually get a bewildered stare, and then proceed to tell them: "You see, any monkey driving a car can run a deer over. That's easy. But it takes skills to maneuver a car in front of a running deer and make the thing kill himself by running your car over!"

And that, folks, is the difference between a Delta operator and a mortal man.

A Child's Hell for a Father's Profit

Platoon photo of me and my Afghan mercs before heading out on
a three-day mission in Jalalabad, Afghanistan.

34

Over the course of my time in service, I have been from one hot spot to another. I have found myself deep inside Iraq, hunting SCUD missiles, to deep within Afghanistan, hunting for Osama Bin Laden. Every deployment was a new experience, and there was nothing routine about combat.

Someone once asked me about combat, wanting to know what it was really like. I replied with, "Combat is long periods of foreboding and solemn thoughts of home, punctuated by moments of stark terror."

Unless you have been there, though, it's impossible to understand. Sure, one can tell you the situation and one can tell you about the emotional side of it, but the person who has never seen combat will never fully get it. That's why I rarely talk about it with my wife or anyone else. The only people I can talk to are those who have been there, those who have seen and experienced combat up close and personal.

It's tough for some to deal with the knowledge of what they have done, what they have seen, without talking with someone who understands. It almost feels as if what we've experienced is not as important as the day-to-day lives of our families or society—so we feel almost disconnected from society.

I was in a small camp in the northern Kunar province of Afghanistan. I had been rotating into this camp for the last two years as a paramilitary contractor for ACES. While I was there, two other Americans and I were responsible for recruiting, training, managing, and leading local mercenary armies into combat in support of the global war on terror (GWOT). One of my responsibilities was to run the mortar section that consisted of 120 mm, 81 mm, and 60 mm gun tubes.

Any time our base came under attack, or there was any sighting of Taliban or Anti-Coalition Militia (ACM), my gunners, which were all Afghans, would drop rounds as directed. They were pretty good for an illiterate, motley, non-English speaking crew. They were quite proficient at plotting enemy positions with a map and a whiz wheel (a circular device used to compute coordinates on a map). This required decent math skills and spatial awareness. My boys could dial in pretty quick and send the first round down range within minutes after an alert. Under my direction, my crew dropped a lot of rounds over the years—I've come a long way from shooting tennis balls out of soda cans.

An observation post (OP), about one thousand feet above the camp, was our early warning system. It consisted of about twenty soldiers secured behind sandbag-roofed hooches made from HESCOS—HESCOS are large sand-filled containers made of cloth and wire mesh. Our OP was constantly getting probed and attacked by the Taliban, and we had sustained several casualties despite having tried everything to curtail the onslaught, including setting up ambushes to interdict the Taliban.

One day, they shot some of our OP guards with snipers about two hundred meters away. I was pissed and had had enough.

We were at about nine thousand feet elevation. I can only describe the mountains around us as scenic; they were much like the ones in *The Lord of the Rings*. The terrain was steep and treacherous. But the Taliban would climb to our OP and use the terrain to attack and conceal their approach, then withdraw.

I took a patrol of Afghans and we went to the OP. I told the OP commander that I was going over the wire with my patrol and placing booby traps on all likely avenues of approach. I was determined to kill these infiltrators and keep them away from the guys guarding us while we slept below.

Besides, I was getting tired of getting up at 4:30 AM to counter a pre-dawn attack with my mortar section. Taliban loved to attack at first light, right after Morning Prayer, or right before last light when they could still see us. Sometimes they would attack in the middle of the night if they could dial in on a light in our camp. Normally, though, all the lights were put out at night, except for red-filtered lights in certain key areas or indoor workspaces. Red-filtered lights are difficult to see from a distance and they preserve soldiers' night vision when they exit into the dark, unlike white lights, which wash out night vision for about fifteen minutes until the eye produces enough visual purple to enable sight in the dark.

I went out with my patrol and had them set and pull security while I went ahead and laid booby traps, using M-67 grenades and trip wire. After I had laid them in, I brought the squad leader and the assistant squad leader over, pointed out where the booby traps were, and made a schematic. We regrouped and moved back to camp.

Shortly thereafter, I went back home to the US, but I returned to the Kunar province two months later. After I got settled in and got a situation update, I asked about the OP and what, if anything, had happened. My contemporary told me that besides killing a goat, the booby traps had killed a young teenage boy when his father sent him into the area to collect unexploded ordnance (UXO) to salvage. The kid had tripped a booby trap and was mortally wounded.

Local workers reported to us that they found his body in our trash dump as he had limped there and died from his wounds. It turns out the father had sent a second son to the same area to continue searching for UXO and he was injured also. The father was admonished and told never to return to that area.

I had to do some soul searching after that report. Man, I had to do a lot of searching. Even today, I wonder sometimes if setting up the booby traps was worth it.

I was told that the OP had come under another attack, and this time they had called in 155 mm howitzer support by indirect fire. The US military laid down a barrage of 155 mm artillery in front of the OP where the enemy would attack from (and where I had laid my booby traps), and as a consequence, many of my booby traps were either detonated or were potentially hanging in precarious positions. I decided to take my patrol back to the OP and remove the remaining trip wires.

At the site, I had the patrol stop short and pull security. I went forward alone because I had emplaced them and knew where they were. Moreover, there was no sense in needlessly risking lives. When I walked down the steep slopes at about 12,000 feet elevation, I had to be careful not to slip and slide through my own trip wires. As I began locating the hand grenades, the hair on my neck stood up when I realized some of these systems just needed a stiff breeze to set them off.

The 155 mm barrage blew the shit out of my traps and now I was in the middle of an explosive mess that could kill me if a bird farted!

I managed to disarm all of the remaining systems and throw the grenades down the side of the mountain. To this day, I'm not sure how the OP faired after I left, because I never returned to Afghanistan after that trip.

This event conjures up memories of a time when my Panamanian-Chinese wife and I were having some quiet time. My wife's English is not the best and her understanding of idiomatic expressions is worse. We were watching TV and the character on screen mentioned booby traps. My wife asked me, "What are booby traps? Do they trap boobs?" Though my wife has a master's degree, this conversation reminded me of how little civilians know about combat and the complexities of warfare.

The Siege in Barg-e Matal

Eating dinner with the troops – Afghan style in 2003

35

About thirty kilometers north of our forward operating base (FOB) in the Nuristan province, several military combat outposts (COPs) were set up in the Barg-e Matal and Kamdesh areas. No more than two platoons of infantry occupied these outposts, and I found it interesting that two of these COPs were sitting in the valleys surrounded by steep high ground. Though they had observation posts on the high ground, they were lightly manned and lightly protected.

In October of 2009, Taliban and ACM breached the perimeter, pushing the surviving American soldiers into a tight perimeter on one side of the camp, and overran Combat Outpost Keating. The US close air support (CAS) came on station and assisted the beleaguered soldiers in the camp. Eight Americans fought valiantly and were killed along with an unspecified number of Afghan police and soldiers. Within a few days, COP Keating was deactivated and all remaining troops were pulled out.

Two other ACES operatives were located with me at North Post. One was the boss, who went by the name Jarad. The other was my contemporary, who went by Levi. We never used our real names and, for the most part, I didn't know anyone's real name—nor did I want to. We did this for personal security and for the safety of our families back home. Levi was a likable fellow, and the Afghan soldiers loved him. He was fair to them and spoke to them like he would to any American. Levi, a former Green Beret, was in his early fifties, and he loved America and his job.

A couple days after I got there, Levi started feeling sick. He complained of malaise, nausea, vomiting, and fever. We just assumed he had the flu or some common Afghan bug that affects us all from the time to time.

I learned early on to avoid eating food at Afghan tables or rugs. The Afghan people customarily eat out of the same pot, digging in with their fingers and plopping rice on their plates. They almost never use eating utensils. They drink from communal glasses and have no problem grabbing a piece of goat or bread and tossing it on your plate. Now, bear in mind, these people didn't even use toilet paper to wipe their asses—they used their left hands and water. They loved to rub their feet and stick their meat beaters into everything without washing their hands. We made it policy, though loosely enforced, that our mercs needed to wash their hands before they ate. If you were watching, they were washing. Otherwise, they defaulted back to their old ways.

The night before, the Afghan troops had invited us for dinner in their dining facility. I made up an excuse for why I couldn't make it. My excuse? I was going to eat American chow and not get sick! Levi thought he had the stomach of a billy goat, so he went to eat with them.

Levi didn't get out of bed or answer his radio for two days. When I checked on him to make sure he was all right—he was laid up like a sick dog. Thankfully, he felt he would be better soon.

Meanwhile, Jarad called me into the TOC and briefed me, saying that we might need to send an advance element to Nuristan, to the COP Lowry, which was still sitting in a deep valley.

These guys were considered Troops in Contact (TIC) around the clock. They had been there for eight months and were never able to send out a combat patrol, because they were too busy defending the camp. Their command decided to evacuate and set a timetable of three days to pull out equipment and men. The problem? They were so engaged with the Taliban, they couldn't dedicate time or men to preparing their equipment for departure. That's where our assistance was needed.

Soon after, Levi felt better and volunteered to go to the COP and coordinate for our arrival the following night. His job was to identify an area where we could ground our gear, configure for missions, and rest.

The following night, Jarad and I arrived with sixty Afghan mercenaries. COP Lowry was only about 150 x 100 meters square. Eight-foot-high HESCOS with concertina wire on top lined the perimeter. A few remote-controlled M-240G machine guns with thermal cameras topped the higher structures, like the TOC. In the center of the COP was a small clearing used as a helicopter-landing zone. It was big enough to support one CH-47 or UH-60 at a time.

Levi greeted us once we landed. The COP was pitch black as he guided us to a holding area where we put our troops. We had a separate hooch to drop off our rucks. We went to the TOC to get a situation report before heading out of the wire. Our job was to leave the wire and actively pursue the Taliban, who were in all of the surrounding villages. The US military would call in helos and load them with equipment while we kept the Taliban back. They had less than seventy-two hours to clear the camp of any US presence. The Talibs liked to hide out in an old abandoned school building about one kilometer north of the camp. We figured we might hit the jackpot if we started there.

We briefed our indige commander on the plan of execution and the time for departure. He assembled his troops and staged them at the COP for movement. At 2200 hours, we left the wire under night optic devices (NODs) and started north on a small dirt road. Levi was still sick and we decided that we couldn't take a sick man along; he was already a walking casualty to us. As a result, Jarad and I, with our band of merry Afghans, went it alone.

36

When we left the friendly line, I was amazed at the amount of flora and trees in the area, not to mention the mountainous terrain. The trees here, as opposed to in the rest of Afghanistan, were dense and tall. The night was clear and humid, and it reminded me of Guatemala, Panama, and even Thailand.

About ten minutes after we departed, the COP came under attack from the south, east, and west sides of the perimeter. As it was landing to pick up equipment, a US CH-47 helicopter was shot down and crashed into the COP.

A single Taliban had been waiting along the southeast wall, and as the helo slowed on a southeast to northwest approach to land, he fired an RPG through the bottom of the fuselage. The round went through, detonated, and blew the leg off a crew chief. This was the initiation for a full attack on the COP.

I saw green tracers from Russian PKM machine guns, AK-47 bullets, and RPGs being fired into the camp. The intense firefight gave Jarad and I pause. We discussed our options with consideration of our mission and the security of the camp, deciding that we would continue north to our objective (OBJ).

It was too dangerous for us to try to cross back into friendly lines at night during a siege. We could have been engaged by the US soldiers in the camp, the Talibs around the camp, or any number of AH-64 gunships that were strafing and firing rockets at anything that moved—the entire valley was ablaze from the rockets.

37

We arrived at the school and, to our disappointment, found no enemy personnel. There was a Taliban controlled village about 2.5 kilometers north, and we headed there to see what we could stir up. Upon arriving, we had to cross a small trestle bridge over a river. We crossed one at a time until we got the entire force across. Security and support teams stayed behind.

We swept through. The usual Afghan dogs were barking and raising hell. Our presence was known. I could see people peering out from behind cracked doors, and others running down the dark streets away from us. I was sure we would make contact. I could almost sense the Talib's presence.

Our stay-behind security reported they had seen a group of what appeared to be fighting-aged males running out of the village and into the hills. Suddenly, shots were fired from behind the buildings on my left flank. Our Afghans returned fire, killing two Talibs. They fell over a ravine and dropped about 500 feet.

Soon the locals started emerging from their houses—the Talibs were getting energized. To my eight o'clock, one of our assault teams entered a house, which resulted in a gunfight inside. No one was killed, but one Talib lost an ear.

As the situation escalated, I found myself isolated with my interpreter—he was known as HD, because of his dream of one day owning a Harley Davidson. We were lying next to a small slope surrounded by mud houses. I told HD to watch our back while I watched the front.

Amidst the commotion, the volume of gunfire was increasing. As people began coming out of the mud houses, someone exited a house in front of me, only fifteen meters away. Because it was pitch black (and we were under NODs), I couldn't tell if it was a man or woman, or if the person was armed. When the person started advancing in my direction, and yelling at me, I saw it was an unarmed woman. I was now concerned that she would continue approaching and distract me, causing me to fall victim to a Talib shooter.

I was trying to work my way back to my Afghans so I could give them maneuver instructions, but first I had to deal with this crazy bitch. I yelled at her to stop, to go inside, and so did HD. She refused, continuing to approach me, yelling as if she wanted to hit me with a broom. I finally fired several shots over her head—no reaction. I lowered the muzzle and fired several rounds in front of her feet. The gravel and sand kicked up, stinging her feet. That got her attention. She jumped and ran back into the house and stayed there until we left.

As fast as the shooting started, it was over. We released the dumbass who was shot in the ear and his two buddies once we determined they weren't Taliban. They had panicked and rushed the door when the assaulters came in and shot what they thought was an advancing threat. We made it back to camp by first light. Everyone hit the sack so we could be fresh for the next op.

38

That afternoon, we ginned up for our next mission that night. We decided to head northwest and lay in an ambush on the road the Taliban traveled to attack the COP. A village sat three kilometers west of the COP and we knew the Talibs were coming from there too. We headed out after last light and started walking along a ravine.

The trail was a goat's trail, only about eighteen inches wide, and covered in wet mud. Water ran down the face of the small mountain, making everything wet and slippery. As we ascended, the drop became treacherous. We walked under NODs and no moonlight along a heavily vegetated trail. The risk of slipping and falling increased with every step.

As HD, my interpreter, walked behind me, I heard him lose his footing, moan, and then fall off the cliff! Fortunately, he landed on a small outcropping about thirty feet below. With my night-vision goggles, I watched as he moved very slowly and deliberately to his feet then brushed himself off and regained his composure before I asked if he was okay. He said, "Yes, Mr. Dale. But I have fallen." *No shit*, I thought to myself.

He started to work his way back up to us, and I could see, under my NODs, a black stain running from his greenish-gray face. Through NODs, everything is in shades of gray and green. The black stain was blood—a lot of it.

When he reached me, I took a closer look at his face. To my shock, I saw a broken tooth protruding out of his bottom lip. I sat him down and called for the medic to patch him up. It was at this point that HD mentioned this was his first mission wearing NODs. I chewed him out for not telling me and putting both his life and the mission at risk. HD was an excellent interpreter and a good

Afghan, though. I understood he was just trying hard to not let me down.

Jarad and I decided this was a good time to hold fast and inspect the trail below for Taliban. About thirty minutes later, we spotted a fire burning on the adjacent mountainside, three hundred meters across from our position. We watched with our optics and determined that these guys had to be Taliban. When we called in for any available aircraft on station, we were informed of an F-15 Strike Eagle patrolling the skies near us. We asked the pilot to use his optics and report what he saw. He came back with, "contact," describing twelve armed Taliban around a fire. We assumed they were using this as their objective rally point (ORP), the place from where they staged their attacks.

We requested immediate air support and rendered the necessary target data. The pilot used his laser to mark the target, and then, from 15,000 feet—several miles—away, he dropped a laser-guided one-thousand-pound JDAM bomb. Time of flight was forty-five seconds and we never heard the aircraft. We watched as the bomb hit them directly, blowing their body parts in every direction.

We headed back to camp—mission successful.

The next day, twelve more Taliban came around the ridgeline in front of the camp during broad daylight. They were looking for some payback and ended up walking into the OP, where those posted there immediately mowed them all down. Twenty-four estimated KIAs in twelve hours! COP was evacuated on time and everyone got out safely. We headed back home and reconfigured for the next rodeo.

On another note, Levi went back to the camp PA and was diagnosed with cholera. He was medicated and made a full recovery.

SEALs—
One Team, One Fight

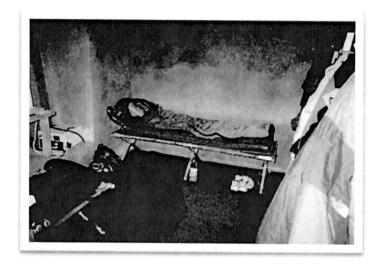

My bed in Russian Compound

39

On my next deployment in May 2010, I ended up in ACES's "North Post" camp in Afghanistan. In total, less than fifteen Americans occupied this camp. I arrived after dark by helicopter. This was standard procedure to protect the helicopter from ground fire. Jeff, one of my counterparts, greeted me and brought me to our housing facility, after which we went into an office where another one of my counterparts, Crazy Mike, was on a laptop watching a video. Knowing I'm a fitness buff, he asked me to watch a clip. The clip showed three young women in great shape going through a crossfit routine that included lifting barbells and other strenuous exercises. Soon after, Jeff volunteered to show me around the facility and orient me to the floor plan.

We went into a small gym where three SEALs were working out—a small SEAL LNO (liaison) element was attached to the camp. I stood in the doorway of the gym, surveying the equipment with Jeff, and had the sudden inclination to say something stupid. Sure that the SEALs could hear me, I asked Jeff, "Are they doing the same fitness training from that video we just watched?"

"Kind of looks like it to me," he responded.

"I don't know, Jeff. It looked like the girls in the video were lifting heavier weights." Needless to say, all the SEALs stopped and gave me a definite go-to-hell look, so I quickly had Jeff show me to my room!

I have many friends on the SEAL teams and we always banter back and forth. At the end of the day, we are all brothers in arms—one team and one fight—I just couldn't help myself. These people were no different. Even though we worked for different sponsors and commands, they still respected me. It was an honor to have them fighting by our side.

Life in the forward operating bases could be pretty comfortable or pretty miserable depending on where you ended up. One of my earlier deployments was to a small, austere FOB in the Kunar. During the Afghan-Soviet war, the Russians occupied this small camp. I slept on a cot in a room I shared with two other contractors. Fleas filled the room, and it was a constant battle to keep them away. If one of us had to take a piss, we had to go outside and walk to the center of the camp and piss into a PVC tube sticking out of the ground. If we had to take a dump, we had to choose from a row of makeshift out-houses less than fifteen meters in front of the 81 mm mortar pit. The shitters had no roofs. This made taking a relaxing dump, especially under the stars and moon, very interesting. It got even more interesting when it snowed (a lot) or rained.

Our mortar section fired around the clock in support of patrols and other satellite outposts around our camp that were in a TIC.

One night, I had to take a shit, so I ran to the out-house. I got nice and comfortable, and started to gaze up at the celestial display of lights in the sky. All of a sudden, the 81 mm mortars firing behind me lifted me off the toilet seat. If you have ever been near a mortar, you will appreciate the deafening sound they produce when fired. It literally scared the shit out of me and rushed me off the toilet.

Life at North Post was pretty cushy. I had my own, if small, room in a Sea-Land container with a bed, a toilet, a shower, TV, Internet, and privacy. We had a great little gym and good food to eat and were in the heart of Taliban country. The latter is what kept our heads in the game.

Lobster Fest

Kunar Province, Afghanistan 2006

40

While at the FOB in the Kunar province, we were planning to hit a target deep in the Korengal Mountains. This particular target was extremely elusive. He tended to leave his house during the day and sleep in a blanket somewhere on the mountain. He was also known to harbor ten to fourteen local and Pakistani fighters at a time. He did this as a security measure. However, we received good intel telling us exactly when he would be home on a specific day, so we planned a vehicle patrol consisting of a three-hour drive through narrow and winding roads up the mountain to his house.

One problem—this area was considered the most dangerous place in the world. US convoys and COPs in the AO encountered the Talibs and ACM there every day. The local population would render alarms to everyone in the province, alerting them that US troops were coming. As a matter of fact, Turbine 33 was shot down in the same area. A quick reaction force (QRF) was aboard when a SEAL team came in contact with the enemy. Turbine 33 was shot down, and then rolled over a ravine, falling another thousand feet to the bottom and killing all aboard.

I had gone on a daylight mission with this SEAL platoon to vet their operational procedures and see if they could do joint operations with us. Some incidents occurred when the SEALs we were working alongside made it apparent that they didn't have the training or experience to handle indigenous soldiers.

Our Afghans were very sensitive to this. Training, managing, and leading indigenous forces into combat is a Green Beret mission. As Green Berets, we trained for this kind of work, which takes a strong understanding of cultural differences and customs. We made our men feel like part of the team, like brothers in arms and not armed servants.

After we conducted final brief-backs and rehearsals, it was time to eat supper. On Friday nights, we always enjoyed steak and lobster. With a belly full of chow, I prepped for departure and drove with one other American and an interpreter in my vehicle.

About fifteen minutes into the drive, one of the lenses on my night-vision goggles (NVGs) failed. I was driving with one eye. Soon after, my other lens failed and I had no back-up NVGs.

We arrived at the target and had to climb down a steep slope on the side of a mountain to a creek at the bottom. We would then ascend the other side of the valley to the target. What should have been a twenty-minute trek turned into a two-hour nightmare.

Walking in total darkness with no NVGs made for a miserable experience. We stopped about halfway down and sat on the slope to take a rest. We realized right away that we were sitting in an area the Afghan villagers used as a restroom. It smelled worse than a Porta Potty, and to top it off, we were literally covered in crap! I always wore gloves in the field, but I'm sure I put my hand in some contaminated soil and then touched my drinking tube at one point.

It was blistering hot and the hike down the hill was exhausting. After about twenty minutes, I was out of water, as were most of the men. My stomach started gurgling and I was getting nauseous. By the time we reached the target and the hit was going down, I was combat ineffective. I sat along the perimeter of the village, shaking with chills, wondering how in the hell I was going to make it back to the trucks. As I sat there, I saw a suspicious bush in the middle of the open area. It must have looked interesting to the ISR above too, because they hit it with an IR floodlight. As this point, all I could do was try to remain conscious and hope I did not pass out and get left behind.

We soon got the call to head back to the vehicles. As we moved out, I walked about ten steps and sat down. I let a few soldiers pass me, and then I stood up and repeated the ritual until I was the last guy and could not get up. The patrol stopped and the two Americans with me came to check on me. They gave me what few sips of water they had and offered to carry my armor and equipment. I refused the drink, figuring someone needed to survive this to tell the story—they would need the water when they had to carry my more-or-less dead ass out of there. As a matter of pride, I didn't let them carry my equipment either. I believe every man should carry his own load, and I had to set the example for our Afghans by never quitting.

Once at the trucks, I got in on the passenger side. I drank some water and opened my vest to cool down. Sweat poured down my face and I started throwing up—rather, I projectile vomited all over the front seat of the vehicle. I apologized emphatically to the American driving and to the interpreter behind me—they were going to have to endure the next two-hour drive enjoying the aroma from my gastrointestinal expulsion. I remember thinking on the treacherous drive back: "God, don't let us get into a TIC."

I was a train wreck. I couldn't see anything and was in no condition to think, let alone fight.

When we arrived at the FOB, my partner, Jay, let me out in front of my hooch so I could recompose myself. Walking to the shower stalls, I looked down at the riflescope and ammo pouches on my chest and noticed what looked like chewed oranges, the little bits you spit out instead of swallow. When I walked into the light, I realized those orange bits were actually lobster chunks from dinner eleven hours earlier! I stepped into the shower with all my gear on and stood there for twenty minutes, rinsing and soaking. It took me three days to overcome the dehydration and fatigue from that night, but I bounced back, ready to do it again.

I learned the next day that the bad guy and his band of fighters had been hiding in a hole covered by the suspicious bush the ISR and I had noticed. I guess we all got lucky that night and lived to fight another day.

Afghan Cowboy

Afghan Cowboy

41

Upon returning to the United States from the Kunar province, I had the opportunity to attend a horseback-riding course. The goal was to learn all I needed to know to ride and care for a horse and to conduct combat operations by horseback. During the one-week course, I learned how to ride a horse and the proper way to feed and care for the animal, including administering medicines if needed. A veterinarian led the training, and he answered all of our questions, regardless of how silly they seemed at first.

One of the questions posed was if it was possible for a horse to get bloat or torsion from eating and then running. Torsion is when the stomach spins on its axis and cuts the flow of stomach contents, a painful and life-threatening condition. If not corrected, the stomach will continue to balloon until it kills the animal, dogs being one of the more common victims. The vet laughed, but answered all the questions with knowledge and patience.

Another student asked what the most efficient way to kill a horse was, if need be. Again, the vet laughed. He didn't think we would ever need this skill, but still supplied the answer: draw an imaginary X from the horse's ears to its eyes, and shoot into the intersection.

During the course, we had two horses die on us. The first was a thirty-year-old nag that suffered from…well, torsion (which should answer the question above for anyone who was wondering). She died a miserable death, and though we had tried to save her, it was too late.

At the end of the course, we were all sitting near a paddock, conducting an after-action review of the week's training. I gazed around, watching all the horses grazing peacefully. The instructor was speaking to us as I thought about the success of the training.

When I glanced back to the paddock, I noticed one horse was lying on its side not moving.

Upon investigation, we realized, to our shock and horror, the six-year-old filly had been grazing up behind an aggressive male and he had kicked her between the eyes, crushing her skull. Blood poured out of her nostrils and from the open wound in her forehead where skull fragments protruded.

She did not die immediately, at least not on her own. After about a half-hour, she started running at full gallop while lying on her side. It was the oddest thing I have ever witnessed. She ran instinctively until she slowed down from exhaustion. I conferred with another ACES operative who was a physician's assistant, and recommended we put the animal out of her misery.

He agreed, so we sent one man up to our vehicles to retrieve a weapon. We had a .22 pistol and a 9 mm Glock in the trunk of one car. The runner came back a few minutes later with the .22 pistol. My buddy, Nick, the lead ACES instructor for the training, decided he would be the one to shoot the horse. When he was offered the choice, I questioned why he didn't want to use the 9 mm. He said he was reluctant to use the Glock, as the .22 would be less messy and still get the job done. He was also concerned that the owner would accuse us of indiscriminately killing his horse. Due to his trepidation, I told Nick to take a before-and-after picture for evidence.

Nick remembered to draw the X and shoot in the center of it. He lined up the barrel and then pulled the trigger. I suppose he was nervous because he jerked the trigger, putting the bullet into the nasal cavity instead of the skull. Less messy? Not so much. Coagulated blood oozed out of the wound, leaving the horse worse off. Her already shallow respiration slowed considerably, but she was by no means dead.

"She ain't dead," I said to Nick. "You have to do it again. Get it right this time." He insisted the horse was dead until I pointed out the rise and fall of its chest. Nick, who didn't want to shoot the horse twice, cursed in frustration. Nevertheless, he manned up, this time killing the beast.

When I returned to Afghanistan a few weeks later, we had around fifteen horses and twenty mules and donkeys at our camp. The animals were there to support Special Operations where they might be needed. All of the horses in the stable were stallions full of piss and vinegar. For some reason, the Afghans didn't believe in castrating their horses; it was prestigious to ride a manly stallion.

There are two problems with stallions—they like to fight each other and they're difficult to ride unless you can intimidate the hell out of them.

During sentry duty, the Afghans rode around the perimeter in pairs, always carrying a big stick, which they used to beat the horses. I noticed the horses were always prancing, throwing their heads back, and seeming energized to fight. The linear pacifier— the stick—seemed to keep them in control a bit, but not enough for my comfort. Since I was now a school-trained cowboy, I went to the stables one morning and decided I was going to ride one of these savages. I thought I had enough experience to handle a stallion. I told the stable hand, an Afghan, to saddle up a horse for me, and he did as requested. I mounted the beautiful black stallion and grabbed the reins. I got a feel for the controls and exited through the gate for what I fully expected to be a leisurely ride.

My mama did not raise a fool, however, so I went out prepared. Before going to the stable and mounting one thousand pounds of muscle and bad attitude, I put on my gun holster with my side arm snug inside. Just in case things got out of hand, I had a 9 mm tranquilizer to level the playing field. As the ride began, the horse was obedient and gave me no trouble. Looking back, I think he was studying me, gauging my experience.

Only a few minutes into the ride, the stable hand came out on his horse, deciding to ride with me. This turned out to be a major mistake. As soon as my horse saw the other, it was game on.

The beast I rode upon lost his mind, trying to fight the other horse with me on his back. I reined him in and attempted everything I knew to control him—nothing worked. He suddenly bolted at a dead run to the top of a hill where we had observation posts and security positions in place.

He dashed through the OP, knocking barrels over, ripping laundry down, wreaking havoc. At first, the Afghan soldiers were terrified, but quickly found it amusing.

I wanted to jump off, but we were going too fast and rocks covered the ground. The horse bucked and rose up on its rear legs. About the only thing he didn't do was breathe fire out of his nostrils!

Finally, he raced down the hill toward the stable in an all-out run. I was scared shitless, but I used to be a professional boxer, so I was known to hit like a truck. I let loose with my fists of fury, punching the stuffing out of the horse's neck to no avail. My foot came out of the stirrup on the left side and I felt myself slipping out of the saddle.

On a side note, their saddles are not made from leather—they're made from wood, and damn did that thing hurt my ass!

I knew I was falling off the horse and tried to jump off, but my right foot didn't slide out of the stirrup in time.

I fell on my back, one leg still attached to the speeding horse, which now dragged me across the rocky terrain.

I was prepared for the situation, as I had already mentally rehearsed what I would do if something like this happened. I went into survival mode, pulling my pistol and aiming as well as I could at the back of the stallion's head. My first shot missed. I was taking a beating on the rocks, but managed to re-acquire my sight.

I started to take the slack out of the trigger and snap off another shot when my foot slipped free of the stirrup. The horse ran to the stable minus one rider.

The stable hand rushed out to get me and insisted I ride his horse. Reluctantly, I got on his beast and asked for the club he had failed to issue me earlier. As I reached for the club, almost like a sick prank, his horse started spinning and bucked me off. Again I found myself on the rocky ground. That was it for me...no more horses—I stuck to pick-up trucks and boots after that.

Up Close and Personal

Desert Storm Feb 1981

42

Not all raids end with tragedy and death. Sometimes they can be quite hysterical. I remember one raid where our mission was to kill or capture a notorious financier of IED attacks on US mil. This guy was responsible for killing many Americans.

By the way, if you notice, I rarely use names, because I do not want these terrorists glorified for what they did. Just know they were evil men and got their just deserts. This particular douchebag was relatively young, around thirty-five years old. He had a reputation of being a playboy, and he was a cocky bastard. He used his money to pay for explosives, and he also paid individuals to detonate IEDs—or themselves—on US military and civilian targets.

We arrived at his doorstep late one night. My assault team stacked the door, and the breacher moved up, placing a small sheet explosive charge on the front door. On the countdown, the breacher command detonated the charge, which had some kick to it. As soon as the charge went, taking the door with it, the assault team entered, with me right on the heels of the number four man in the stack.

We entered the living room and then bolted for the master bedroom. Shrapnel and splinters from the charge were embedded in the adjacent wall, and probably would have killed someone standing on the other side. As we entered the master bedroom, we found, to our surprise, our Baghdad playboy in bed with a woman. Both were naked, enjoying themselves. He paid no regard to the explosion, or the fact that we had entered his bedroom and interrupted his romantic interlude.

I stopped next to his bed and leveled my HK-16 at his head, yelling for him to get up. That son of a bitch looked at me and held his hand up as if saying, "Give me a second. I need to finish first!" Then he pointed to the woman under him, raising his eyebrows as if to say, "Come on, look at her. She's hot! Let me finish because this might be the last time I see her!"

Though I was amused, his complete dismissal of us pissed me off. My boys snatched his naked ass out of bed, and I covered up the naked woman.

We found weapons and large amounts of money, which he'll never see again. At this point, I would have rather shot him to save some room in the detention center, but we flex-cuffed him and hauled him off with us. As for the woman; it looks like she had a new apartment. It only needed a new front door, Spackle, and some paintwork.

Some missions were routine, and some—like the previous—were humorous. Others, like the one during my next trip to Tikrit, were heartwrenching for me.

On this particular trip, I was working with a small ACES team, supporting the military in its effort to find Saddam Hussein. The unit was preparing to conduct a daylight raid on a target who was considered an extremely bad guy with ties to Syria. His neighborhood was large with two-story homes and what can only be described as townhouses. My job was to travel into this neighborhood alone to conduct a close target reconnaissance (CTR). In my recon, I needed to positively ID (PID) the target's home and confirm his car was parked in the gated driveway. I would then report to the unit and lead them on to the objective.

I admit I was a bit nervous about traveling alone into this neighborhood in broad daylight. Anything could have happened. My truck might have broken down, I could had a car accident, or vigilante insurgents in the area could have stopped me. I made it through safely, though, and was able to PID the target and his car.

After going back and rendering a quick intel update, I led the unit to the target.

To my chagrin, the target's red car was gone. I was concerned he had left and that I would look like an idiot. I stopped my truck in front of the residence, and the unit operators quickly assaulted the house.

I jumped out of my truck to assist where I could. Right away, I saw a three-year-old boy standing at the gate of his father's (the target's) house. The boy screamed in horror.

The poor kid was watching a bunch of Americans—in full combat kit and carrying weapons—kick in his dad's front door. When I saw the look on his face, the tears in his eyes, and heard him scream, all I could do was think about my children. What if it was one of them? I instinctually, or paternalistically, picked up the boy in one arm, leveling my weapon at the neighbors with my other arm. I tried my best to comfort the little guy, assure him all would be okay and that we would leave soon.

For some time after that, my heart was torn. I often thought about that boy and how terrified he was. While his father was in our custody for interrogation, I grew furious with the man. Why did he put his family in peril? Why did he involve them by operating out of his house? I will never understand. Nevertheless, through extensive interviews with him, he revealed information that ultimately saved many American lives. His life was spared and he was handed over to the Iraqi authorities for prosecution.

Afghan Moon

Marksmanship Training

"The good fighters of old first put themselves beyond the possibility of defeat, and then waited for an opportunity of defeating the enemy."

—Sun Tzu

43

The Afghan soldiers were an interesting lot. I tried hard to understand their culture. And just when I thought I couldn't be surprised by anything they did or said, I would be taken aback by another "WTF" moment.

I distinctly remember having an Afghan working for us who, though a Sharia lawyer at one time, had changed his loyalties to the US. He seemed like a smart guy who always rendered good intelligence reports. He was highly respected by everyone.

One day, the man walks into our office to discuss something with us. At first, I just gave him a cursory glance and listened to what he had to say as relegated by the terp. When I swiveled around in my chair to respond, I saw the strangest thing ever. This guy had threaded a sewing needle and taped the end of the thread to his eyebrow so that the needle would dangle in front of his left eye.

He had a sty in his eye and according to Afghan tradition, or medicine, this was a surefire way to make the eyelid infection go away. The really amazing thing was that this guy actually believed this. He walked around all day wearing this silly "medical" appliance!

On another occasion we had captured a Taliban fighter, and during his detainment, the guy was asked a series of questions about his mission and associations. He pretty much clammed up and didn't say anything, because he knew that all he had to do was be silent for seventy-two hours and he would get plenty of rest and food, and then be released thanks to policies mandated by certain people in our government.

My partner got frustrated and he told the Talib: "You don't know who you are dealing with. We've put men on the moon, so don't think we can't extract information from you!"

The Talib, who was a simple, uneducated man from the country, sneered and replied: "You cannot put men on the moon." He held up his hand and extended his index finger and thumb in front of his face about two inches apart. "Because the moon is only this big!"

The sad thing here is that these simpletons were kicking our asses with the basics. Of course, US policies had severely hamstrung our efforts to be effective; nonetheless, these guys were winning.

What Americans sitting in their living rooms don't understand is that winning is relative. If we engage the Taliban and kill fifty of them, and they kill only one American, the Taliban will believe they've won! In their eyes, chalking one up in the win column would be called for.

Why?

Their belief system tells them they will go to heaven and receive seventy-one virgins (plus or minus one virgin, depending on who you ask) when they die. They accept death more readily than Americans. They know that if we lose one man, it becomes a national policy debate that eventually will influence our combat operations.

I am of the opinion that surgical strikes have little effect on their resolve to fight. In fact, I have heard it said that they think we're cowards because of them. What the Afghans and Iraqis do respect is blunt trauma. You kill a handful with a predator, they think, "So what?" You level an entire village, now that gets their attention. They are a different breed of warriors. They don't see war as an extension of politics; they see it as a life-and-death struggle irrespective of the political consequences or public sentiment.

We fight with boxing gloves and they fight with tire irons and bad intentions. Our soldiers are the best in the world, but if our government doesn't slip the lead, they will only be as effective as our conservative war-fighting policies, which brief well in Congress, and sound good to the anti-war activist, but do nothing to save American lives on the battlefield. We have reached a point in the war where soldiers are required to knock on the enemy's door during daylight hours and ask him to surrender. We have reached a point where enemy personnel are detained and then released after seventy-two hours because they refused to speak and we have no recourse to extract information. On more than one occasion I have captured the same insurgent twice. The war, much like Vietnam, is being fought by politicians and armchair quarterbacks at the expense of American lives.

After my last rotation out of Afghanistan, I was assigned to another mission in another part of the world. It was a welcome change of pace and scenery. While on deployment in South America, I worked with indigenous mercenaries. We call them mercs, for short. They're tough sons of bitches, and quite capable. We train them to do a vast array of tasks to hone in their combat skills. These mercs already have the warrior instinct; they just need more training, better tactics.

We had a mission to recover a black satchel. It contained an external hard drive and call rosters for Islamic terrorists operating in this specific country. I won't say exactly where, for my own safety.

The mission was to travel into a terrorist enclave, hidden in a quiet neighborhood. You wouldn't know the place from any other upscale neighborhood in the States. It had long, winding roads; driveways riddled with dozens of types of trees.

There were dogs on every corner.

Speaking of dogs, I'll stop for a moment. I have a love-hate relationship with them. I *do* love them, but they're no good for a mission. Damn things can ruin any covert operation as quick as anything can. There's nothing worse than a yapping dog when you're trying to sneak around at night.

This place had a shit-ton of them, and I wasn't happy about this. Still, we made our way.

Within this neighborhood, we searched for a specific house. It was a compound, really. Large, lots of ground to cover. We'd break in and recover the black bag. We knew we had good intelligence; we knew the bag was still there. We also knew this: At just the moment we grabbed it, terrorist cells around the world would be alerted. They'd change phones, handsets, and security contracts and activate protocol emergency plans. They'd do all this in a heartbeat to avoid being compromised.

We had to make this look like an inside job. Sneaking in undercover wouldn't be a problem. This was only one of hundreds of covert missions I'd been on. The area was overrun with Arab immigrants, so we wore ankle-length black thaubs to imitate what most men would be wearing. The flowing thaubs allowed us to hide a ton of weapons and never be second-guessed.

Especially at night, no one would realize we weren't from the Arabian Peninsula.

We wore long sleeves as opposed to the short ones. I had a throwing dagger strapped to the side of both arms. I loved shit like this. When it was all done, a courier would be accused of being a traitor. A rival terrorist cell would be accused of having the bag. It would cause a little inter-rival battle, a bit of chaos for a month or so, but when they figured out it was us, it would be too late. We would have all the information we needed.

The whole operation was to be quick, in and out. We didn't carry radios, earpieces, or anything, having previously determined that all contact would be through hand signals.

We pulled up to the front gate of the compound in two cars and a van. There were twelve of us in all. One guy took the lead with a Hooligan Tool. Then another with a thirty-five-pound, all-metal battering ram.

We entered the compound and went straight to where we thought the bag was. These guys were all the same. They might as well have left us a map to the bag. We found it in a locked suitcase secured to a water pipe with a cable and padlock. They had it hidden in what was marked as a janitor's closet.

The battering ram did the job to bust the door open, and any alarms that went off did so too late. Once we had the bag, I took a quick inventory of the contents and found two hard drives, several passports, a phone roster, and four CDs.

We were in and out in seven minutes.

And we never even heard a dog bark.

This was my kind of shit!

We stayed the night in a safe house ten kilometers from the neighborhood. It was operated by the local intelligence service, and from what we knew, only one guy, Carlos, the chief of the department, occupied the safe house.

Carlos gave us sanctuary and a place to hole up until the morning when a helicopter would pick up the bag. Then we'd head back to the US.

We dropped our gear in Carlos's office, where we intended to sleep. The perimeter was secure, but despite the lack of visible threats, I posted two guys on lookout. With some of these jungles having the most corrupt security in the world, you never know who you can trust.

Carlos invited us to go with him to get a bite to eat at a local cantina. He told us it was safe to leave our gear and that we didn't need weapons.

We agreed to go, but not without some of our things. We brought sensitive radios, crypto, and most importantly, the black bag. Along with these things, concealed pistols were a minimum for guys like us. I wasn't about to be completely vulnerable on what could be the "streets of Laredo," and risk getting shot, robbed, or kidnapped, or having our hard-won trick-or-treat bag stolen.

Once we were packed and packing we headed out to eat. Two of my guys were tired and stayed behind, which I was happy about since I wasn't keen on walking back into ambushes either.

We got back around 2200 hours, dropped kit, and prepped to rack out for the night. It was then I noticed the black bag was still in its original place. I walked over and picked it up, realizing it never got packed. The man responsible must have overlooked the bag when he was gathering the radios.

I checked the contents and accounted for everything, but I went to sleep with an uneasy feeling.

The next morning we put the bag on the chopper and off we went. Mission complete. Or was it?

A few days later, Seth, the senior operative, and I went to headquarters to speak with the mission commander.

"Did we find the golden egg?" I asked. I was eager to find out what kind of intelligence we gleaned from the bag.

He looked at me. "There was nothing in the bag."

I looked at Seth. He had this whole, "Who ate the canary?" look on his face. Without saying anything, we reached the same conclusion. Carlos lured us away for dinner, and one of his men came into his office to copy and clean the hard drives, CDs, phone roster, and passports. My two guys must have been out on patrol, thinking the black bag was with me.

Shit! I thought. That son of a bitch snaked us good.

Seth and I remained silent. We still had to determine whether the intelligence was really compromised. Perhaps we had misplaced the contents in another bag. Or anything else that we hadn't thought of.

Back at the safe house, it didn't take long for us to realize something was amiss. We went back to the commander and I insisted that the items were in the bag when we put it on the helicopter.

Two months later and we were still looking for this stuff. We knew we hadn't screwed up. We didn't screw up; *I didn't screw up!*

I confronted the FBI agent who was responsible for pulling the intelligence from the contents of the bag. On our insistence, he checked the bag again.

Goddamn! There it was. All the missing shit was sitting pretty in the bag's outside pockets.

That lazy son of a bitch had done a cursory check and then tossed the bag into the corner of his office. The intelligence that we extracted was now two months old and probably useless!

Seth and I were glad we dodged that bullet and weren't canned for the epic fuck-up. I was just starting to think that my days working under the government were coming to an end too. I had to put my trust in too many people who weren't out putting their asses on the line every day, and I learned a valuable lesson: sometimes you just have to chalk it up to luck.

Donkey Turds and Warthogs

High Altitude and low Opening

44

On my next rotation back to Afghanistan, I visited a small COP in the southern part of the country, near the Pakistani border. This camp only had one Special Forces A-Team and about thirty local Afghan recruits. I was there with two other ACES operatives to discuss combat operations in their area of responsibility (AO).

These guys were getting hammered constantly by 122 mm rockets and mortars. At one point, they were ambushed repelling an attack, and lost one Green Beret and several Afghans. The joke, which had a lot of truth to it, was that AQ and Taliban used this camp to train their fighters.

After conferring with the ODA (Operational Detachment Alpha) commander, we decided we would assist by running combat ops in the AO. Our first mission was a helicopter insertion at night about one kilometer away. We landed and then moved off through a valley lying in a patrol base on the top of some high ground.

The mission was a three-day dismounted patrol in the ODA's area to look for enemies and collect intelligence. The scenery along the area that bordered Pakistan was amazing. The large chasms filled with steep mountains and green valleys reminded me of the Grand Canyon.

On the first morning, I awoke at about 4:30. The sun was already up, and my Afghans had already risen and prayed to Mecca, and were prepping for the next leg of the movement.

Now, my boys were more like urban warriors than tactical field soldiers. They spent most of their time assaulting buildings, compounds, and homes in the cities. They were like a high-speed SWAT team with a military flair, so this particular unit was way out of its element when I took them on a three-day combat patrol.

However, all of the food, ammo, water, and comfort items they needed were in their backpacks.

The previous night we only moved for about four hours and two kilometers before we set in our patrol base, so these guys shouldn't have drunk a lot of their water. They should have been fresh enough to continue humping the hills. When I sat up and looked around—I had already given the order to the commander to "saddle up" and be ready to move in thirty minutes—I saw something that really got my attention.

Several of the soldiers were pouring their drinking water on their heads and hands to bathe, and I noticed that many were wearing their heavy polypropylene underwear under their uniforms.

At this point, I came unglued at the seams! I jumped to my feet and yelled for the commander and all of the squad leaders. What were they thinking? These men were using precious drinking water to wash after only eight hours in the field! I reminded them that no resupplies were coming and that we were in an area void of water. I walked over and checked some of the men's rucksacks.

Now I was really amazed! These guys had brought shampoo, soap, shaving gear, and all kinds of shit they didn't need.

I have gone several weeks in the field, jungle, desert, etc., without changing my uniform or bathing. After about three days in the field, everyone stinks and you don't even notice anymore. I rarely wore underwear, T-shirts, or socks, and the only hygiene that I practiced routinely was brushing my teeth every day. As long as my mouth was clean, I felt good.

After giving them a lecture in the field about the errors of their ways, I "suggested" they remove their heavy poly-p underwear because we were about to start humping some serious terrain, and they would overheat and dehydrate faster if they kept it on.

Some heeded my advice. Others couldn't see beyond the fact that they were cold now, but in a few minutes they would be sweating their ball sacks off. In the end, I decided that today was "training day" and that some were going to learn a hard lesson.

We began moving down a steep hill. By the time we reached the bottom, these boys were hurt'n units! Some had no water left; others were microwaved in their comfy poly-p.

I continued on point to lead the patrol, passing a small puddle of dirty water with goat and donkey turds in it. I thought about how a dog wouldn't even drink from that sewer and continued walking. Then, it got very quiet behind me. So I stopped, turned, and looked. I'll be damned if these knuckleheads weren't on all fours drinking the water like dogs!

I yelled at that them to stop, but it was too late. I issued a stern-ass chewing to the commander, telling him this was not going to work well in a couple of hours.

We finally picked up our pace and climbed a very steep mountain. When we reached the top we were on a plateau overlooking some majestic scenery—it was awe-inspiring. I noticed old rock fighting positions from the Soviet-Afghan war and I had to reflect on what it was like for the Russians fighting here. I told the men to stop, face out, and take a ten-minute break.

That break turned into a several-hour-long hurling and diarrhea fest!

Five Afghans had gone down hard from the dirty water. They shit their pants and blew chunks all over that hilltop. My American counterpart and I did what we could for them, which wasn't much since we didn't have any meds with us, and then just sat back and waited until the shit storm and hurling fest subsided.

Though many were still sick, the show had to go on. We couldn't sit too long or we would risk getting attacked or falling behind our extraction time.

We managed to survive the three-day patrol by redistributing water and better managing our movement distance and travel times.

On the night of day three we were extracted and went back to base to reconfigure for the next mission in this AO.

The follow-on mission had us landing at 0100 near an unoccupied and dilapidated mud compound that would act as our MSS (Mission Support Site). From it we would run all of our combat ops in the AO. We were on high ground and could see the ODA camp about a kilometer west from our position. We had received intelligence that the ODA camp was going to come under siege that night and we were expecting a Taliban force to travel to a known rocket POO site (Point of Origin) to fire their rockets at the camp.

Our plan was to drive two Humvees the ODA had loaned us to a vehicle drop-off point (VDO) in the vicinity of our planned ambush site. We were hoping to interdict the Talibs as they moved to the POO site and kill or capture them.

When our two helos landed we only had to walk about one hundred meters to the compound. I had sixty Afghans with me and five other Americans. The Afghans made up a heavy weapons section that included a 12.7 mm or .51 caliber DSHK Russian machine gun and three Chinese 82 mm mortar tubes.

The plan was to occupy the MSS under the cover of darkness, cover the weapons, and not offer any sign that we were there. Like for most missions, we needed the enemy to remain ignorant of our presence. So we got the men in the MSS and, with the exception of our sentries, I had everyone bed down until first light about three hours later.

Around 4:30 AM I heard some movement in the camp as men prayed and others became restless. I was still lying on the ground with my head resting on my rucksack when one of my terps came to me with a question.

He said, "Mr. Dale, some of the men would like to go down the hill and bathe."

I sat up and asked him, "What did you say?" We had walked a hundred meters that night and these guys felt so "yucky" that they needed a bath? After a moment, I said, "Walid, you now have my undivided attention. Tell me more about why these guys need to take a bath in a combat zone with bad guys around while we're trying to remain stealthy."

He went on to explain that the five guys concerned were all sleeping in one small cluster along the wall about twenty meters from me. He said that the Quran requires that if a man has a nocturnal emission, also known as a wet dream, that he bathe and cleanse his body.

It took me few seconds to register what he had just told me. So I said to him, "Walid, are you telling me one of the soldiers woke up this morning, realized that he had a wet dream, and then shared that info with the other four next to him? Are you telling me that the other four woke up and exclaimed to each other that they too had wet dreams?"

What are the chances that five men cuddled together all had wet dreams in the same night?

At this point, Walid was getting flush in the face and very uncomfortable with the conversation and my line of interrogation. When I asked him the question, How did five guys snuggling up with each other all have wet dreams? I almost felt like he wanted to scream and run out of the MSS, yelling, "I can't take it anymore!"

Homosexuality was commonplace in Afghanistan, although they didn't want to admit it. In fact, they had a saying that went like this: "Girls are for babies, and boys are for fun." Personally, I didn't care about their sexual preferences, as long as they didn't try to include me in their fun. In fact, I quite admired these guys because, although they would walk holding hands and carry AK-47s to the bedroom, they could fight like some badasses when it was trigger time!

It didn't take a genius to figure out what was going on there. That morning these five butt-pirates had an orgy, albeit a quiet one, and now they wanted to get all religious on me and take a bath. I was pissed and disgusted at the same time. But, out of respect for the customs and religion, I told Walid to organize a security patrol and take those men down the hill to bathe in the dirty run-off water on the side of the road. That was all that was available.

I told him, "This conversation ends here! You tell those lover boys this is a combat op. They better get focused, and if that shit happens again, someone is going to lose pay after I break my foot off in their ass! And, NO, I won't let them bathe after that rectal violation!"

Later that afternoon, the Special Forces team brought us two Humvees. One was a standard utility vehicle, kind of like a pick-up truck, with two rows of bench seats in the bed. The other, which I ended up driving, was an up-armored Hummer with an M-2 .50 caliber machine-gun mounted in the turret.

We received an updated intel report from their 18 Foxtrot Special Forces intelligence sergeant. We agreed that we would leave just after sunset and drive to the VDO, about seven kilometers away, on a circuitous road. At around 1800, it was still daylight and I instructed the unit to prep for tonight's mission.

I was taking twelve Afghans with us. They would ride in the back of the utility Hummer. The driver was another ACES operative. The other three passengers were American. One was an Air Force JTAC; the other an Army Ranger. JTAC (Joint

Tactical Air Control) is a designation granted to those personnel who have the training to call in close air support. We were all qualified to call in emergency close air support (ECAS), but when a school-house trained JTAC calls in close air support, the pilots feel a little more comfortable—they get that warm and fuzzy feeling that comes with knowing there likely won't be mishaps because of some procedural mistake.

The other American with me was a medic who I called "Doc." Doc had a lot of combat experience and had been ambushed many times. It was pretty much understood that if you went out with Doc, you would get into a firefight. He was like a bullet magnet, except tonight he would attract RPGs.

As I stood in the MSS, prepping gear and loading my GPS with coordinates and waypoints to the ambush site, I heard the distinct sound of a rocket motor overhead.

About four seconds later, the first rocket hit the camp with the Green Berets. I couldn't believe it—a daylight attack with rockets was unusual; my thought was that these Taliban were emboldened because the ODA camp was so remote that CAS never challenged them.

As soon as the first rocket impacted, another was flying overhead.

It was game on, and we had missed the opportunity to ambush the attackers.

Change of plans: I loaded the troops and told them we were heading to the planned ambush area, and to be prepared to hit them on their egress.

Now, it turns out there was a second POO site firing from west to east and one firing east to west, a ground assault coming over a hilltop to the south of the camp, and a forward observer (FO) position on a hill to the north calling corrections for the rocketeers. At this point, we had still gone unnoticed.

As we were scrambling to load vehicles and move, we decided to initiate a response on the eastern POO site about 1 kilometer away and on the FO position about 1.5 kilometers away. We fired the 82s and a Dishka, leaving one ACES operative in the camp to direct fires and provide support for us if we got in trouble.

By the time we left the wire it was dark. To my chagrin, the IR lights failed to work on both vehicles. We were driving under NODs with no moonlight and it became almost impossible to drive without colliding into large rocks. To make matters worse, I was driving the lead vehicle and trying to see through bullet-resistant glass, which only made things tougher, and because of a weak signal, I had to hold the GPS out the window to navigate. The trails were washed out and many looked like dry streambeds. Because of all the factors against us, we missed our waypoint and had to turnaround. Meanwhile, the fight was still on. Rockets rained down, and the ground assault element was engaging the camp from the high ground.

I finally found the turnoff and we headed north. The trail was tight and now it was impossible to see. I ended up breaking light security and switched on my white lights to avoid driving off a ravine. It was a risky decision, but I was left with no alternative. Shortly thereafter, we hit a dead-end and we were channelized in the streambed with large boulders on both sides. It was then that an RPG sailed across my hood and exploded next to my vehicle about five meters away.

I heard the ACES operative in the second vehicle yell out to his Afghans: "Shoot, God dammit, shoot!"

By this time we were in full counter-ambush mode. The Ranger on the .50 let off a short burst when the gun jammed and stopped firing. The JTAC was calling in for ECAS, and Doc, who was sitting next to me, started egressing the vehicle to take cover and fight.

Every gun we had, minus the .50, was running and firing 360 degrees…it was an impressive demonstration of firepower.

Amidst all of the excitement and rush to clear the vehicle, I had to do several things at once. First I needed to kill the white lights. Because the light toggles were on the same panel as the ignition toggle and I couldn't see, I killed what I thought was the lights and instead turned off the ignition.

As soon as I could, I killed the lights. My foot was on the brake, but the Hummer was still in drive. I opened the door and grabbed my SR-16 and M-79 grenade launcher (a Thumper), and as I started to exit simultaneously with Doc, I let my foot off the brake and the vehicle lurched back. Doc's ankle was pinned between the bottom of the armored door and a boulder.

Once I'd freed him, I reengaged the brake, realizing I needed to put the vehicle in park to keep it from rolling back. I got out and immediately started returning fire with the Thumper. Doc suffered a broken ankle, but he never complained or said a word until later when he took his boot off at the ODA camp.

My first round landed right on the mark of where I thought the attack was coming from and then it was all over.

While in the Army I used to carry an M-203 grenade launcher attached to a CAR-15 and I became very proficient at shooting the launcher using a technique called "sensing" instead of the sites. The technique is analogous to spraying water out of a water hose. You just know from the arc of the spray where the water will splash down. Because I experientially knew the capabilities of the 40 mm grenade, its max ord and range, I was able to dial right in with a first-round strike about two hundred meters up a hill.

At this point we had to get the vehicles turned around. When we finally did, we had the Afghans walk on foot to provide security for our slow movement.

The JTAC was still on the PRC-117 radio and switching back and forth to the MBITR PRC-148 radio, calling for close air support. We got a reply from a flight of A-10 Warthogs who were thirty minutes out and reported they were on their way. After forty minutes and no-show of the A-10s, we called and asked them for their new ETA.

They informed us they had gone back to Bagram Air Base to refuel.

My question to the JTAC was, When were they planning on telling us they weren't coming right away? They didn't know what kind of trouble we were in, and we may have been counting on their help.

Finally, about an hour and a half later, they were overhead. It took them three hours to drop the first bomb. We kept giving them enemy locations and they kept hesitating because they couldn't see personal weapons (at night) at 10,000 feet. I was getting frustrated because the FO position didn't need weapons, just a radio to call corrections for the rocketeers. Moreover, the pilots didn't need to see weapons to engage—that was my call. Geez, I was getting so pissed that some guy in an airplane was afraid to fight because he might get in trouble.

One of the pilots informed us that, because we were less than 1500 meters from the Pakistan border, he was reluctant to drop his ordnance. I told the JTAC to inform the pilot that he was the weapon and I was aiming the sights and pulling the trigger—he needed to do his job and keep us from getting killed. Fuck Pakistan and hurting their feelings because we dropped bombs too close to their border—they're not Americans and we are! All I cared about was making sure that our Afghan soldiers and we, as Americans, didn't die because of some arbitrary rule that sounds good but is completely useless.

Finally, the A-10s released their ordnance and started killing the enemy. As soon as they effectively started engaging, the Talibs retreated toward the Pakistan border.

Shortly thereafter, the lone ACES operative at the MSS reported that a low-flying fixed wing aircraft had flown from the Pakistan border and circled his position once before flying back to the border. After a seven-hour fight, it was over and we linked up with the ODA at their camp where we conducted an after-action review and rendered a SITREP to our higher. The next day we headed back home to reconfigure for the next rodeo.

The Final Ambush—My Epiphany

Post assault assembly prior to movement back to the camp.

"The bravest are surely those who have the clearest vision of what is before them, glory and danger alike, and yet notwithstanding, go out to meet it."

—Thucydides, c. 471 BC

45

I went back to Afghanistan in the summer of 2010, assigned to another FOB in the northern Kunar province. It was a small US-controlled military base used to support tactical operations. Knowing I was coming close to my retirement, I thought it was going to be a pretty easy job, but that was never guaranteed. We were still in a heavy combat zone, and raids took place often. As of late, though, the days and nights had quieted.

One night we decided to run a patrol to link up with another US patrol coming in from the south. We were going to meet them halfway and exchange some much needed radio and medical equipment.

The plan was to head out at 2000 hours and drive for three hours. Then we would wait. The other patrol was three hours away, a little farther than us, the terrain from here to there a little rougher, but we didn't expect our wait to be long.

We radioed them on our departure from the FOB, and the southern patrol acknowledged they were leaving the wire. After an hour, we received communication from the other patrol informing us they were delayed. The southern patrol had to reload their radios with new crypto.

We arrived at the designated link-up point with twenty-three vehicles, mostly Toyota pick-up trucks covered in desert and net camouflage. Gun turrets and sniper blocks lined the back. My truck was a comm truck, fitted with what seemed like a thousand antennas that basically screamed "target."

The southern patrol was at least two hours out, which left us sitting on a road with a north-south running river seventy-five meters to our east, a mountain ridge to our west, and no other direction to drive except south or back north. We stopped our vehicles and established a security perimeter.

Our Afghan interpreters listened to the ICOM radios that the Taliban used and kept an ear out for any chatter. At this point, we had sent another six vehicles forward two kilometers south to conduct the link-up with the southern patrol. Within minutes, we heard the enemy come up on the net and start hatching a plan of attack. The Taliban commander started directing his elements to set up ambush lines and emplace IEDs to the north over the same road we had just traveled down.

The Taliban controlled this area for a ten-kilometer stretch. Along the side of the road were numerous burned-out hulks belonging to fuel trucks, re-supply trucks, and military vehicles that had been destroyed by the Taliban in order to choke off our supplies to the north. The road was known as a heavy combat zone, but it was the only route choice we'd had. It was unsettling knowing we had to sit here for another two hours, while our enemy was making plans to ambush us.

Every so often, the Taliban would fire a volley of PKM 7.62 mms at us to solicit a response. We maintained weapons discipline and did not return fire. The Taliban could not see at night. With zero illumination, they couldn't pinpoint our location. They were probing us with direct fire so we would compromise; fortunately, our Afghans were trained well and were smart enough to figure out what was unfolding around us. They maintained noise and light discipline and did not shoot back. The Taliban were close, but not close enough to do any damage.

Because we knew this was going to be a fight and we were going to have to run a gauntlet, we started planning our strategy. We had called in for air support and we were able to garner two Apache AH-64 gunships. All other air assets were committed to other ops that night, so we would be short-handed in air coverage.

We decided the most tactical and logical thing for us to do was to turn the vehicles around and make a run for it, back north, as soon as we had completed the mission. We would use the Apache gunships to provide top cover and clear the road to our front. We were running out of time. At 0400, the sun would come up, and we would lose our night-vision advantage.

At 0200, our lead patrol effected link up with the southern patrol and exchanged equipment. On the way back to our position a kilometer away, I could see the southern patrol heading back as they drove through an open area below us.

I watched as they were ambushed at close range. There was nothing we could do but dispatch the Apaches in their direction and fend for ourselves as we headed back north.

The Apaches were already on station and ran south to provide close air support. We watched helplessly, as we hadn't come under effective fire yet, and called in a situational report to the southern patrol and our FOB to the north, alerting them to the situation. Our Quick Reaction Force had been standing by at our camp and prepared to roll in support of us.

It was a spectacular sight. The lead patrol was running and gunning with explosions from RPGs and the AH-64's rockets illuminated their vehicles. When the lead element linked up with us, they had suffered a few casualties, including their medic who had a gunshot wound to the stomach. We tended to the casualties and then notified the AH-64s of our plan.

It was now 0300 and the witching hour was almost upon us. The AH-64s called us and announced *"Bingo"* and *"Winchester"*, informing us they were out of fuel and ammo and needed to fly south to rearm and refuel at the FOB where the southern patrol originated.

The Apaches cleared the area and we finalized our plan as we waited for them to return. We listened to the Taliban commander brief his fighters and reassure them of victory. The southern ambush element was moving toward us on foot, planning to hit us from the rear. We were enveloped from the north, west, and south, with the river to our east. Shit was getting serious.

The dirt road we were on was rough; it was not so much a road as a thousand-year-old farmer's path. The fastest we could expect to drive over it in our decked-out vehicles was about five miles per hour, any faster and the vehicles would have been destroyed and shit would have fallen off, including our soldiers.

The Taliban commander directed his men to fight from close range, less than fifteen meters from the road.

They were going to run in between our vehicles. This would serve two purposes: first, it would render the AH-64s ineffective because the Apaches couldn't shoot that close to us. Second, it would be a challenge for us to shoot them between trucks and not get hit by crossfire. This was a ballsy tactic on their part and a big departure from their usual tactic of fighting from afar.

These sons of bitches wanted to jump on our trucks like Apache Indians jumping on a stagecoach. Hell, they were so confident that they discussed how many weapons they would recover from us after they had won! At one point, I wondered if they'd be taking scalps. That's how fucked up those sons of bitches were!

The Taliban commander told his men to lie low because we were waiting for the AH-64s to return. He knew that we would lead out with the Apaches and then run the gauntlet behind them. This guy had experience and knew what he was doing. I just wondered if his men had enough grit to carry out his plan.

The Apaches returned and conducted a strafing run in front of us, which was our signal to go. I was the fifteenth vehicle in the formation, and my vehicle was easily identifiable by all of the external radio antennas, which indicated that I had a command vehicle—*just great.*

I watched as our first truck pulled off at a "blazing" speed of five miles per hour. As soon as he departed all hell broke loose.

Every gun on his truck was lit up in the fight. Then the second truck left, and then the third, and so on. We maintained a fifty-meter interval between trucks, so we were spread out over one kilometer. We estimated the ambush line to be three kilometers long on a winding road with a sharp Z-pattern making it ideal for a classic L-pattern or Z-pattern ambush.

Basically, we would wind around one corner only to be hit again on the next. The Taliban soldiers would be able to cover the entire distance with half as many combatants as they would need to cover the entire stretch if it had been in a straight line.

As our trucks rolled out, I couldn't believe that, despite all of the ambushes and battles I had survived, I was about to deliberately drive into one, knowing two IEDs were waiting for us. I closed my eyes and took a deep breath. I could see the faces of my four kids, my wife, and my parents. They were what I cared about most in life. Yet here I was risking everything, and for what? This could be the last time I would see them, even if just in my mind's eye.

It was at that moment that I realized that after twenty-nine years in this line of work, and having survived every campaign from Grenada to Afghanistan, I needed to hang up my guns and go home. It was time. I had to enjoy the rest of my life with my family. I loved my work, but as the years came and went, I was tempting fate more each day and was sure I would soon meet my end if I didn't graciously bow out.

I made peace with myself and opened my eyes. If I was to get home, I would have to get through this first. I put on my game face. It was time to get it on and not be distracted by personal thoughts; I needed to stay switched on and tuned in. I dropped the truck's transfer case to low and four-wheel drive. I told my terp,

Naim, who was behind me, to point his AK-47 out the window and kill anything that moved. "Put out your cigarettes and hold on to your hats because here we go, boys!" and off we went. Five fucking miles an hour. Woo-hoo!

So many guns were firing that it sounded like an Army Infantry Division in contact. Bad guys were running on the road and spraying away with their second-hand automatic weapons and pin-shooter handguns, strafing trucks and sand. They were hardly an elite corp. I was driving with one hand and shooting my pistol with the other. The way the truck was bouncing, I was lucky that I didn't shoot a hole in the door, or worse, shoot my own leg.

We passed the corner of the first elbow in the road veering east. This is where we anticipated the IEDs were planted. Nothing happened and we continued to roll and fight.

I blew the shocks on the front ride of my truck and the tire was rubbing inside the wheel well. It rubbed hard and long enough that it caught fire. But I beat that flaming horse and made her go, on fire or not.

As I rounded the second elbow in the road back north, a Taliban fighter appeared on my side of the road and made a run for the truck from about five meters away. At this point, I laid the pistol under my right butt cheek so I wouldn't drop it on the floorboard. I needed to free up both hands so that I could muscle the steering wheel to the left. The Taliban fighter coming at me stumbled as he was taking a shot with his AK-47, which caused him to launch a stream of bullets into the dirt alongside my truck. This serendipitous moment allowed me to gain purchase on my pistol. I pulled it out and insulted his face at point-blank range with a controlled pair of 9 mm Hydra-Shok bullets. He slammed back to the ground; errant rounds from his AK-47 flew off harmlessly.

As we cleared the ambush, the Taliban commander was admonishing the IED triggerman and asked why he didn't detonate the two IEDs. The triggerman replied that he couldn't because of the volume of fire coming his way: he'd been afraid to lift his head to see the target vehicle!

We finally made it out of the ambush and back to camp, suffering several wounded but no casualties. The Taliban completely destroyed one vehicle and damaged eight others. When we pulled up in front of our TOC, the headquarters' staff and a team of Navy SEALs were waiting for a SITREP. I rendered a data dump, checked on the troops and wounded, accounted for equipment, and then went to bed and slept for the rest of the day. My ass was beat and I just needed some sleep.

As I collapsed onto my bunk, I knew this would be my last mission. I'd been fighting for too long.

Stars Earn Stripes

Stars Earn Stripes

46

Who'd have ever thought that once I retired from combat, and moved on to Hollywood, I'd relive the same horrors? And on a Hollywood production set no less. Yet this is exactly what happened.

I had two such experiences. One was the helicopter crash. The other was during the filming of NBC's reality show, *Stars Earn Stripes*.

I was paired with a man named Terry Crews, who I grew to love like a brother. Terry is one of the most humble, honest, and benevolent men I've ever had the pleasure of knowing. I could sit for hours listening to him, mesmerized by his stories. Over the course of a few weeks on set, he told me about his wife and kids, his childhood, his pro football career, and his acting career.

I returned the favor, telling him my own stories—of family, of my military career, and of my thoughts on Hollywood. We'd spend countless hours talking about life, and we became quite good friends. We were called "Killa Grandpas" by some, a moniker that we earned because we were both grandfathers, yet built like twenty-year-old bodybuilders.

This was my first Hollywood experience, so I wasn't quite sure how everything would go. But our first episode was to conduct a helocast insertion, which is right up my alley. Helocast is the term used for an infiltration technique—usually some form of water infiltration—where a helicopter flies at a slow hover, about six feet over water (or land), and soldiers jump off.

In this case, the infiltration was to be by a rubber inflatable boat with a motor, called a RIB. We were supposed to jump from the bird and swim approximately one hundred meters to the boat, climb aboard, and then move to a beach-landing site.

Sounds easy, right?

Before we started the mission, Terry informed me that he wasn't a strong swimmer. I appreciated his candor up front because it allowed me to improvise some floatation devices for him.

I took a couple of empty water bottles—let's call them improvised buoyancy compensators—and stuffed them in each cargo pocket to give him some added buoyancy. Shit, I wasn't sure they would work at all, but I needed to do something if we intended to complete the mission together. I figured even if they didn't, they might psyche Terry up enough to make him think they were helping him.

He and I had a pre-mission strategy briefing to discuss contingencies. I assured Terry that he had nothing to worry about and that I wouldn't let him drown. I promised him that I would remain close and if he got in any trouble, I would grab him and tow him to the boat.

I gotta tell you here, Terry weighed 238 pounds to my 210. After we strapped on kit and weapons we both were about thirty-five pounds heavier. To exacerbate the problem, the gear had no buoyancy whatsoever. Once we were in the water, the vests and load-bearing equipment were like lead-filled weights. After about two minutes in the water, I noticed Terry was barely treading, and making no headway.

At that rate, I knew he wouldn't make it. It was a matter of seconds before he would start struggling. I turned back and swam to him, at which time I saw the frantic arm sweeps of a man just keeping his head above water.

Within a matter of seconds, I was upon him, grabbing the back of his body armor and beginning to tow him. I could tell knowing he was not alone brought Terry some mental and physical relief.

As I pulled, I realized I was expending an inordinate amount of energy. I was growing concerned that I would not be able to continue much longer before I, too, started to drown. Since one arm was committed to towing, I only had one arm to keep myself afloat. Moreover, my weapon had spun around from my back and was now dangling between my legs.

While trying to stay afloat, Terry and I kicked at each other, and our arms, legs, and weapons became enmeshed, creating a real problem for both of us. After a few minutes, Terry began to panic and flail. I had to release him because he was starting to pull me under, and though I am an exceptionally strong swimmer, I couldn't stay afloat and hold him up at the same time.

Terry went under and then bobbed back up. I tried to reengage him but he was getting too frantic. Suddenly, the water bottles I placed in his cargo pocket popped out and surfaced in front of him like buoys. When Terry saw the bottles, he panicked even more. I guess he figured that the loss of bottles meant that he was doomed. At that point, he threw his arms up and just let go, putting all his faith and trust in me to keep him from drowning.

Meanwhile, I had waved in the safety boats. Within seconds, the boats arrived and plucked him out of the lake.

Just in the nick of time!

And I was left to "Charlie Mike" (Continue Mission) on my own.

Hot Latin Wrath

My badass wife

47

I returned home and was fortunate enough to sell the security consulting company that I had started in 2004. I put my formal resignation in to my government employers and started working as president of my old company, which specialized in high-risk facilities like nuclear power plants and petro-chemical plants. I work from home but I travel a lot. However, the places that I go are "low-lead" environments and I'm no longer living on the edge every day.

By January 2012, I had fully retired from combat duties and was happy spending time with my family. My life was now void of six-month or yearlong stints fighting rebels and mercenaries. I was always home and my beautiful Panamanian wife didn't have to sit around worrying about whether I had made her a widow and my kids fatherless.

One night while I was away on business, my wife and three-year-old daughter were home alone. At 2230 hours on a weeknight, while taking a shower, my wife heard an alarm across our intercom system that indicated someone had entered our locked home on the bottom floor. She ran into the bedroom and grabbed my Bushmaster AR-15 equipped with double-stacked, thirty-round magazines, visible laser, an Aimpoint sighting system, and a rail-mounted gun light. She called my cell phone and ran to the landing on the second floor of our three-story home when she heard the intruder moving toward her on the bottom floor.

Over the phone she told me she was scared. I reassured her and told her not to think when she saw the threat, but to press the trigger until the threat stopped. With our daughter, who was asleep at the end of the hall on the second floor, in mind, my wife decided to maintain her defensive position. As she yelled at the intruder and threatened to kill him with her rifle, she hit the panic button on our alarm and the intruder ran out through the garage, which he'd come in through.

As it turns out, the intruder knew I wasn't home and cloned my garage door opener, which facilitated his entry. What he did not anticipate was that the house was armed with an alarm system and a mother who was not afraid to kill in order to save her daughter's life.

Two weeks later, while I was on a business trip, another intruder attempted to break in through the front door at 1730 hours. He was gutsy doing it in broad daylight.

His entry was delayed due to a chain securing our double doors. My brave wife once again armed herself with the Bushmaster and dissuaded the intruder from coming in. After the local SWAT team, which had been monitoring my house more closely since the last incident, had arrived and cleared my home, one of the officers told my wife that she would have been within her rights to defend herself and my daughter.

My wife angrily responded that she had "no problem shooting his head off." Her problem was that she didn't want to have to clean up the mess afterward!

Now, why did my wife use an AR-15 assault rifle? Simple—it's her second amendment right. Moreover, the range she may have had to shoot from could have been up to thirty feet from her defilade.

For a novice shooter, a long-barreled weapon with a laser is far more accurate than any handgun under those conditions. Furthermore, she didn't have to mount the weapon in her shoulder, and because of the laser and gun light, she could have simply shot from the hip. Lastly, in the event that she missed, she had two thirty-round magazines filled with hollow-points to increase her chances of stopping the threat. I was proud knowing that my training had paid off and that my wife had the fortitude to defend our home and family while I was gone.

My world had turned over to more of a consulting role, which included assisting with books, movies, TV shows, and classroom training. I was enjoying it. It never occurred to me that what I thought was simply useful knowledge made me a subject-matter expert for the rest of the world. I was highly regarded, and it was happening fast.

I received a call from the producer of the Discovery Channel's *One Man Army* asking me if I was interested in being a part of the show. I said yes and underwent the screening. I remember undergoing a series of written psychological evaluations and an interview with a psychologist. It seemed like they were very concerned with violence and the potential for fighting with the other participants in the show. I told them that, although I am a former professional boxer, kick boxer, and mixed martial arts fighter, I am also a responsible parent and a professional who doesn't fight except in self-defense. In the end, I got the part and made my television debut in September 2011, competing against a SEAL, a Ranger, and a Marine. Seeing me as a large threat, the three competitors decided to gang up on me and remove me quickly. Nonetheless, I lost the challenge with grace and my head up. It was because of this great showing that NBC contacted me and asked me to be on their reality show *Stars Earn Stripes*.

The Roadster Warrior

Vale Tudo (anything goes) fight in Norfolk VA 1996

48

After the Discovery Channel show was filmed, I went back home to Panama City Beach. I was leaving the gym one morning and decided that I needed to swing by the bank, which was about a thirty-minute drive away. As I was driving, I came up behind a pick-up truck. I noticed a pit-bull, a shotgun in the window, and that the driver was wearing a wife beater T-shirt and baseball cap. As soon as I finished my observation, he threw a beer can out of the truck and hit the hood of my BMW. I came unglued and honked my horn, flipped the bird, and let loose with a volley of choice expletives.

The man immediately pulled over as did I. I got out of my car to have a meeting of the minds with this idiot. As soon as my 210-pound body emerged from this tiny BMW Roadster, his eyes got big and he sped off. About ten minutes later, I came up behind a string of cars and this same pick-up truck was three vehicles ahead. He saw me through the rear view mirror, pulled over, let the other cars by, and then cut me off. He pulled out a pistol and aimed it at me as I started to get out of my car and then sped into a trailer park.

I ducked behind my car and then pulled into the front of the trailer park and called the police. I told the cops I would wait in front for them to file a report. As I waited, this lunatic came back and parked diagonally behind my car. He had a baseball cap on sideways, gold chains, and a lot of bad attitude.

I walked toward his vehicle and informed him the police were on the way and that he could deal with them. He looked at me with this crazy look and said that he was going to kill me and he just wanted to know whether I wanted to be stabbed or shot. I backed away from his truck and decided to memorize his back license plate. This guy had taken the time to cover his license plate with a piece of paper before he returned to jack with me. I reached down, pulled the paper off, and quickly memorized the plate number at which time he jumped out of the truck and attacked me.

I ended up beating this guy into oblivion, literally, because we were alone and I felt that if he got the upper hand, he could kill me. His first mistake was that he underestimated me. I hit him so hard that I broke my left hand as his ear exploded with blood. His second mistake was that he wore his britches below his hip and they fell to his feet, thus hobbling him and making him a stationary target. It was like working out on a heavy bag. I hit him with a series of combinations and then pulled his shirt off as I was trying to gain purchase to hold him up for more punishment. He finally fell over after I hit and kicked him with no less than one hundred strikes. From the dilated pupils and his fidgeting, I could tell this guy was gooned out on methamphetamines, thus why he was able to take such a beating, but he finally went fetal on me and cried for me to stop.

Five police cars with officers drawing guns, two ambulances, and a fire truck arrived at the scene. They handcuffed him immediately and began patching him up. They walked me to my car and noticed that I had a Special Forces decal on my car. In front of the other five, one of the officers asked me what had given me the right to approach his car. I couldn't believe what he had just asked me and I was pissed! I told him my right to defend myself takes precedence over law. I said, "That guy should consider himself lucky because I have killed a lot of men for a lot less. Today, I just happened to be unarmed. Usually I'm armed, but not today; otherwise, the outcome may have been more severe."

My attacker, realizing the error in his ways, quickly and adamantly apologized for what he had done and took full responsibility. The police officer asked me if I wanted to press charges and I told him to give me a minute. I looked at the guy lying on the ground disheveled, pants to ankles, no shirt, covered in blood and dirt, and crying, and I asked him, "Hey, did you learn a lesson?"

He replied, "Yes, sir. No one has ever beaten my ass the way you did, not even my father, and I am truly sorry, sir!"

I looked at the police officers and said, "No charges, I think he gets it now and I gotta go run errands." One of my fingers is still crippled from the incident, but at least no one was killed.

What the hell would the producer of the Discovery Channel show think of this? Yeah, I fought back in self-defense, but with a guy like me, self-defense can really fuck someone up.

Microcosmic Warrior

Kickboxing at Light-Heavy weight before turning to Pro Boxing in 1998

49

My mother and father didn't teach me to be a coward, nor did I teach my kids to be so. I had many rules in my house and none of them were negotiable. My kids were never allowed to say, "I can't." My wife and I never told our kids that they couldn't do something or that it was "too much."

I wanted my kids to know life is about choices. We choose who we want to be and we choose who we don't want to be. I could have been an astronaut, but I chose to be a soldier. "I can do anything" is my attitude, and with it, because I actually believe it, I am empowered. With every success, with every victory, I am more empowered. With every failure, I become more resolute to attain success.

When I was a teenager, I used to dream of becoming a professional boxer. I really liked the style of Sugar Ray Leonard. I used to box in local tough-man contests, I fought in martial arts tournaments, I fought in the street, and, hell, I fought in my sleep. I loved the art of hand combat, still do. It is the most basic form of war. It is war in a microcosm—man on man. It gets no more primitive than that.

I've been a student of the martial arts since I was thirteen. By this time, I was a seasoned fighter who rolled on the playground, the bus stop, the front yard, or at the Sadie Hawkins Dance with every bully that came along.

I liked bullies. There is nothing like beating down a bully in front of all of his friends and then having the girls chase you for the rest of the school year. Okay, girls weren't my motivation…well, not entirely. My real motivation was my will to win and my desire for self-preservation. When I fought, or fight, it was a battle to save my life. Because, in my father's words, which still resonate in my mind, losing is not an option.

194

While in the Army, I continued to train in martial arts and I would go to the Fort Bragg boxing club to train with Coach Brad and some of the fighters there. My trainer and mentor, Jim "Smokey" West, was by far the most influential man in my martial arts journey. Jim was a Green Beret with mad fighting skills.

The first time I met Jim, I went home and had a nightmare because of him—the man is a scary fighter. I often say he's like a modern-day Wyatt Earp, without guns. If you go against Jim, you will lose, and you will lose badly. Through Jim's teaching, my son and I both earned second-degree black belts, and my daughter earned her second-degree brown belt. Some reading this may say, "So what? Anyone can earn a black belt." Well, not anyone can earn their stripes the way we did.

Traditional schools have their students perform katas, forms, and light sparring. Black belts are usually required to teach and demonstrate proficiency in these skills. Not at Jim's school. Because Jim was a performance-based teacher in a performance-based school, katas and forms were given no time. Sparring...not really. When it came time to test, my kids, Jim, and I would go to another school and, behind closed doors, without an audience, we would engage in an all-out street fight with an opponent from that school of equal or better stature.

As a father, I was proud to see my thirteen-year-old daughter hold her own and beat a black belt in a girl-on-girl no-holds-barred test. My son earned his first-degree black belt by the time he was seven.

I earned all of my belts in all-out combat. Sparring with foam gloves is a foreign concept to me. Remember what I said before, "We train the way we fight, and we fight the way we train." Fighting with foam gloves (where you just tap each other for points) teaches bad habits and a false sense of effectiveness. I lost my first fight to five teenagers because I pulled a kick to my opponent's head and tapped him just like people do when sparring in school. He grabbed my leg and down I went—game over. They whooped my ass; I learned a lesson. If I kick someone in the head today, out of self-defense, I am aiming for the fence and hitting a home run.

When both of my kids asked to learn martial arts, I told them I would allow it; however, once they started they had to stay with it until they earned their black belts. It was like going to school—there was no quitting or days off. My son did try to quit once, but as a father, true to my word, I made him keep up with it, and in the end, he earned his second-degree black belt.

I started boxing on the pro-boxing circuit while in the Army assigned to Special Forces. I boxed at that level for three reasons: it was a childhood goal, I trained hard enough that I was good enough, and I wanted to reach the pinnacle of excellence. I knew I couldn't be a world champion or anything more than a journeyman being in SF, married, the father of three kids, thirty-two years old, and a college student, but the point is that I had set a goal and I would be damned if I didn't follow through.

Be All That You Can Be—
Victors or Vanquished

My Family

Bodybuilding, May 2012

50

We live in a "what's in it for me culture" that puts self-interest and greed over the good of the nation. Our young people are taught by government and the Utopia seekers that others are responsible for our mistakes or inadequacies—there is no personal accountability.

You have a choice in life: you can follow and be guided like a donkey or you can lead like a stallion and blaze your own trail in life.

To be a good leader one must know what it is to follow and know when to take the lead. Leaders never waver; they maintain their poise when all else is in disequilibrium.

I have always considered myself an athlete. As a kid, I found sports to be a great outlet for my energy. They kept me from indulging in stupid stuff like taking drugs, breaking the law, or sitting on my ass eating potato chips and getting fat. In my mind, strong men don't take drugs to feel good about themselves, raise their self-esteem, or help them cope with the trials and tribulations of life. Real men (and women) overcome adversity through strength of character, effective intelligence, and the desire to rise above their peers and superiors. Through personal victories, one can raise his self-esteem, and consequently, others will see his strength and admire him for it. Drug abuse is not admirable. It lowers one to the level of quitters and the weak minded, and ultimately causes one to become a grazer, a sheep, who always gives way or succumbs to the meat eaters in this world. I am a meat eater, I lead before I follow, I take what is mine, and I feel solace in knowing that I can take what is yours if I want it.

I am empowered through my will and my strong character.

As a father, I mentor my children by setting the example...a positive example. I remember when we used to drive together in my pick-up truck to go to karate practice. I would take that time to teach my kids something rather than to talk about useless shit like what some jackass was doing on MTV, or whatever drama was happening between kids on the playground.

I wanted my kids to remain above the social fray and look toward being superhumans. I would pick any subject, like science, sociology, or whatever was of interest, and I would teach them what I knew. Young minds are fertile and you can fill them with shit or you can enrich them with critical thought. I chose the latter, and my kids' minds and bodies have flourished to excellence.

My daughter, Danielle, was an honor-roll student, a second-degree brown belt, class president, captain of the varsity cheerleading team, and homecoming queen. She went to college and earned two bachelor's degrees in business and marketing. Today she is a successful entrepreneur who can pave her own way through life without a handout.

Like any father I wanted a son who would be like me, at least the good side of me. I used to work out with my son when he was a teenager. We would go running together and lift weights at the gym. After about two years of training with him, he became an excellent runner and won many track events at school. He ultimately became the team captain for track and soccer. He was the class president in his senior year in high school and went to college on an academic scholarship. He was a straight-A student the entire time he was in school except for a total of five Bs he received in band class and choir.

I say: "So what, maybe my kid can't sing and dance, but he sure as hell can outthink you, outrun you, and kick your ass!"

He went on to be a bodybuilder and competed in his first bodybuilding show at twenty-two as a heavy weight.

He joined the Army after college and now is undergoing training to be a Green Beret medic and ultimately a Delta operator.

My wife is also a bodybuilding figure competitor. She competed in her first show the same year that my son did.

I was more into cardio and lifting for functional fitness. But it soon occurred to me that I should train to compete too so that one day we could all compete in the same show together. I started training in earnest, and eight months later, my son, my wife, and I all competed in Orlando, Florida, at a state-level show.

One of my greatest memories is of posing next to my son on stage as heavy weights and walking with a fifth place medal while my son walked with a sixth. My wife also earned fifth place.

We jumped on stage with our A-games with well over two hundred competitors, most seasoned, and we held our own and came out in good standing. Since then bodybuilding has become a family staple that keeps us focused on our health and minds. It is a family affair that bonds us tightly.

For me, personally, bodybuilding and athleticism have opened a lot of doors in my Hollywood career. I instill the winning attitude that my father passed down to me into my thirteen- and three-year-old daughters. My thirteen-year-old is an exceptional soccer player. She began training with her brother when she was only four. Now, at thirteen, she is a stellar athlete who trains with me every day in bodybuilding.

Her goal is to compete as a junior bodybuilder when she is sixteen. She is one hell of a fighter too. Every evening after our gym workout, we conduct MMA training. I awarded her a purple belt at the early age of seven. Like her dad, she can hit like a truck and I have no doubt she will one day earn her black belt.

My three-year-old recently started learning the one-two punch. I am cultivating a specific mindset within my daughters: I do not want them to ever feel inferior or weak. My mission in life is to be the best father I can, and to raise my children to be strong, independent, and confident adults. They will never be victims.

In March of 2012, NBC contacted me and asked if I was interested in participating in a reality show called *Stars Earn Stripes*. They discovered me through *One Man Army* and thought I was a good fit for their show. All of the winnings would go to military charities, which to me is a great cause, so I agreed.

I was paired with Terry Crews. I had an amazing time hanging out with him, and learned a lot from this American. He is by far one of the most humble and decent men I have ever met. In fact, all of the cast and operatives on the show were exceptional Americans with their hearts in the right place. *Stars Earn Stripes* has resulted in many opportunities for me, which I hope to take advantage of and use to represent the military in a very positive light. Particularly, I want to represent the Special Operations operators and the Delta Force, who are part of America's secret army and fight and die every day on behalf of all Americans. They are men whose names and deeds will forever go unspoken in the name of national security and selfless sacrifice.

My life has just begun and I have only closed the first chapter. My life is a work in progress, grounded in the desire to mentor our misguided and lost youth and stand against those who live in deceit and dishonor, and who work toward diluting our men to social eunuchs and extinguishing the American way of life.

How do I define myself? America first! Integrity, honesty, courage, justice, and loyalty. "With every victory I am empowered and with every defeat I am more resolute…I will never quit!"

I want young Americans to know that life is about choices and a series of compromises. The road you travel can be that of the majority, it can be the road less traveled, or it can be one you blaze for yourself in order to be your own man.

CPSIA information can be obtained
at www.ICGtesting.com
Printed in the USA
LVOW12s1921220516

489467LV00005B/378/P